Georgia Legal Research

CAROLINA ACADEMIC PRESS
LEGAL RESEARCH SERIES

Suzanne E. Rowe, Series Editor

Arkansas Legal Research
Coleen M. Barger

ટ&

Florida Legal Research, Third Edition
Barbara J. Busharis & Suzanne E. Rowe

ટ&

Georgia Legal Research
Nancy P. Johnson, Elizabeth G. Adelman, & Nancy J. Adams

ટ&

Illinois Legal Research
Mark E. Wojcik

ટ&

Michigan Legal Research
Pamela Lysaght

ટ&

Missouri Legal Research
Wanda M. Temm & Julie M. Cheslik

ટ&

Oregon Legal Research, Second Edition
Suzanne E. Rowe

ટ&

Pennsylvania Legal Research
Barbara J. Busharis & Bonny L. Tavares

ટ&

Tennessee Legal Research
Sibyl Marshall & Carol McCrehan Parker

ટ&

Washington Legal Research
Julie Heintz

Georgia Legal Research

Nancy P. Johnson
Georgia State University
College of Law

Elizabeth G. Adelman
University at Buffalo
Law School

Nancy J. Adams
U.S. District Court
Northern District of Georgia

Suzanne E. Rowe, Series Editor

CAROLINA ACADEMIC PRESS
Durham, North Carolina

Library of Congress Cataloging-in-Publication Data

Johnson, Nancy P.
Georgia legal research / by Nancy P. Johnson, Elizabeth G.
Adelman, Nancy J. Adams.
    p. cm. -- (Legal research series)
Includes bibliographical references and index.
ISBN 978-1-59460-388-4 (alk. paper)
    1. Legal research--Georgia. I. Adelman, Elizabeth. II. Adams,
Nancy J. III. Title. IV. Series.

KFG75.J64 2007
340.072'0758--dc22
                                                    2007021260

CAROLINA ACADEMIC PRESS
700 Kent Street
Durham, North Carolina 27701
Telephone (919) 489-7486
Fax (919) 493-5668
www.cap-press.com

Printed in the United States of America.

Nancy P. Johnson dedicates this book to the students of Georgia State University College of Law, who made her a better researcher.

Elizabeth G. Adelman dedicates this book to her family: Robert, Lily, and Jacob.

Nancy J. Adams dedicates this book to Mary Ann Neary, who introduced her to the world of legal research.

Summary of Contents

Contents

List of Tables and Illustrations

Series Note

The Legal Research Series published by Carolina Academic Press includes an increasing number of titles from states around the country. The goal of each book is to provide law students, practitioners, paralegals, college students, and laypeople with the essential elements of legal research in each state. Unlike more bibliographic texts, the Legal Research Series books seek to explain concisely both the sources of state law research and the process for conducting legal research effectively.

Preface

Georgia Legal Research is designed to aid law students, attorneys, and law librarians in acquiring and perfecting legal research skills. In addition to explaining Georgia legal research sources, it focuses on research strategy. Since the researcher has a wide range of options for locating primary and secondary materials, we include both print and electronic sources. Throughout the chapters, we refer to commercial providers of computerized legal research, primarily Casemaker (free to members of the Georgia Bar), LexisNexis, Loislaw, and Westlaw. We also include online subscription services offered by private publishers and Internet websites maintained by the Georgia government.

The text begins with an overview of the research process and legal analysis. Each chapter states the learning objectives for the different resources. They include an explanation of research strategies and a discussion of print and electronic resources. To simplify the research process, we often include checklists of various research tasks. We also provide selective sample pages and screen shots to illustrate the sources. Some chapters include appendices that provide the researcher with more detailed information.

Each chapter gives a very brief explanation of appropriate federal materials that could be used with Georgia materials. Since legal ethics research is very important, a separate chapter addresses that topic. At the end of the book, there are three helpful appendices: Georgia and national citation rules, a bibliography, and a list of Georgia practice materials.

Acknowledgments

Professor Suzanne E. Rowe, the Series Editor, greatly improved the quality of this book by reviewing each chapter. Moreover, as the author of previous books in this series, Professor Rowe shared freely from her own body of work. In this regard, the authors acknowledge Professor Rowe's significant contributions to Chapters 1, 8, and 11, and to Appendix A.

The authors are grateful to research assistants Kelly Fahl and Jeff Hinman for final proofreading.

The authors acknowledge Thomson/West for granting permission to include reprinted materials from *Winning Research Skills* (2006-2007). The authors also acknowledge the Georgia State University Law Review, LexisNexis, Thomson/West, and Yahoo! for granting permission to include images of their products and services.

The authors also wish to acknowledge support for this work from Georgia State University College of Law, the University at Buffalo Law School, and the University at Buffalo Libraries.

Georgia Legal Research

Chapter 1

The Research Process and Legal Analysis

After reading this chapter you will:
- understand the intersection of legal research and legal analysis;
- recognize types of legal authority;
- be familiar with the Georgia and federal court systems; and
- have an overview of the research process.

I. Georgia Legal Research

The fundamentals of legal research are the same in every American jurisdiction, though the details vary. While some variations are minor, others require specialized knowledge of the resources available and the analytical framework in which those resources are used. This book focuses on the resources and analysis required to be thorough and effective in researching Georgia law. It supplements this focus with brief explanations of federal research to introduce additional resources and to highlight some of the variations.

This book is not designed to be a blueprint of every resource in the law library or search engine on the Internet; many resources contain their own detailed explanations in a preface or a "help" section. This book is more like a manual or field guide, introducing the resources needed at each step of the research process, and explaining how to use them.

II. The Intersection of Legal Research and Legal Analysis

Most students realize in the first week of law school that legal analysis is difficult. At the same time, some consider legal research simplistic busy work. The basic process of legal research *is* simple. For most print resources, you will begin with an index, find entries that appear relevant, read those sections of the text, and then find out whether information that is more recent is available. For most online research, you will search particular websites or databases using words likely to appear in the text of relevant documents.

Legal analysis is interwoven throughout this process, raising challenging questions. In print research, which words will you look up in the index? How will you decide whether an index entry looks promising? With online research, how will you choose relevant words and construct a search most likely to produce the documents you need? When you read the text of a document, how will you determine whether it is relevant to your client's situation? How will you learn whether material that is more recent changed the law or merely applied it in a new situation? The answer to each of these questions requires legal analysis. This intersection of research and analysis can make legal research very difficult, especially for the novice. While this book's focus is legal research, it also includes the fundamental aspects of legal analysis required to conduct research competently.

III. Types of Legal Authority

Before researching the law, you must be clear about the goal of your search. In almost every research situation, you will want to find constitutional provisions, statutes, administrative rules, and judicial opinions that control your client's situation. In other words, you are searching for primary, mandatory authority.

Law is often divided along two lines. The first line distinguishes primary authority from secondary authority. *Primary authority* is law produced by government bodies with law-making power. Legislatures write statutes; courts write judicial opinions; and administrative agencies write rules (also called regulations). *Secondary authority* includes all other legal sources, such as treatises, law review articles, and legal encyclopedias. These secondary sources are designed to aid you in understanding the law and locating primary authority.

Another division is made between mandatory and persuasive authority. *Mandatory authority* is binding on the court that would decide a conflict if the situation were litigated. In a question of Georgia law, mandatory or binding authority includes Georgia's constitution, statutes enacted by the Georgia legislature, opinions of the Supreme Court of Georgia, and Georgia administrative rules. Georgia Court of Appeals decisions would be binding on trial courts within the appellate court's jurisdiction. *Persuasive authority* is not binding, but may be followed if relevant and well reasoned.

Within primary, mandatory authority, there is an interlocking hierarchy of law involving constitutions, statutes, administrative rules, and judicial opinions. The constitution of each state is the supreme law of that state. If a statute is on point, that statute comes next in the hierarchy, followed by administrative rules. Judicial opinions may interpret the statute or rule, but they cannot disregard them. A judicial opinion may decide that a statute violates the constitution or that a rule oversteps its bounds. If there is no constitutional provision, statute, or administrative rule on point, *common law*, also called judge-made law, will control the issue.

IV. Court Systems

Because legal research includes reading judicial opinions, researchers need to understand the court system. The basic court structure includes a trial court, an intermediate court of appeals, and an ultimate appellate court, often called the "supreme" court. These courts exist at both the state and federal levels.

A. Georgia Courts

Under the Georgia Constitution, there are seven classes of courts.[1] In addition to the Supreme Court and the Court of Appeals, judicial power vests in superior courts, state courts, juvenile courts, probate courts, and magistrate courts. The four latter courts, also called trial courts, have limited jurisdiction. Limited jurisdiction is the authority given by law to the various courts to rule on certain types of legal cases. Each of Georgia's 159 counties has "at least one superior court, [a] magistrate court, a probate court, and, where needed, a state court and a juvenile court."[2] There is no reporter for trial court opinions.

A 1906 constitutional amendment established the Court of Appeals of Georgia as a supplementary appellate court.[3] This court exercises appellate and *certiorari* jurisdiction in all cases not reserved to the Supreme Court of Georgia or conferred on other courts.[4] Such cases include civil claims for damages, child custody cases, cases involving workers' compensation, and criminal cases other than capital felonies. Although the Supreme Court has *certiorari* jurisdiction over all decisions of the Court of Appeals, the Supreme Court exercises this jurisdiction sparingly, usually in cases of great public importance.[5] The official reporter for the Court of Appeals is *Georgia Appeals Reports*.

The Supreme Court of Georgia, established in 1845 as the highest court of review, exercises exclusive appellate jurisdiction in cases involving the construction of a treaty, the constitution, the constitutionality of a law or ordinance, and election contests.[6] The Supreme Court also exercises general appellate jurisdiction in cases involving title to land, equity, wills, habeas corpus, extraordinary remedies, divorce, alimony, questions certified to it by the Court of Appeals, and

---

1. Ga. Const. art. VI, § 1, para. 1; *see also* Judicial Branch of Georgia at www.georgiacourts.org/courts.
2. Ga. Const. art. VI, § 1, para. 6.
3. 1906 Ga. Laws 24.
4. Ga. Const. art. VI, § 5, para. 3.
5. Ga. Const. art. VI, § 6, para. 5.
6. Ga. Const. art. VI, § 6, para. 2.

Table 1-1. Georgia Court System

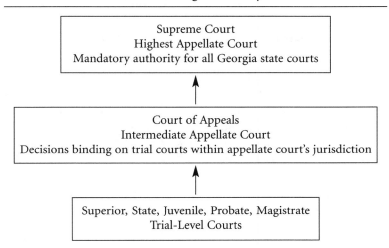

cases in which the State could impose the death sentence.[7] The official reporter for the Supreme Court is *Georgia Reports*. Table 1-1 shows a graphical display of the Georgia court system.

B. Federal Courts

In the federal judicial system, the trial courts are called United States District Courts. There are ninety-four district courts in the federal system, with each district drawn from a particular state. For the state of Georgia, there are three districts: southern, middle, and northern. Notable cities in the various districts include: Savannah in the southern district; Macon and Athens in the middle district; and Atlanta in the northern district. Each district serves the residents of many counties since Georgia has 159 counties. You can find federal district court cases in the *Federal Supplement*, although only a small

---

7. Ga. Const. art. VI, § 6, para. 3.

percentage of district court cases are published. The opinions that are reported are precedent-setting opinions. You can find unpublished cases online.

Intermediate appellate courts in the federal system are called United States Courts of Appeals. Twelve of these circuits are based on geographic jurisdiction. In addition to eleven numbered circuits covering all the states, there is the District of Columbia Circuit. The thirteenth circuit, called the Federal Circuit, hears appeals from district courts in all other circuits on issues related to patent law and from certain specialized courts and agencies. You can find federal courts of appeals cases in the *Federal Reporter*. A map showing the federal circuits is available at www.uscourts.gov/links.html. Circuit maps may also be found in the front of the *Federal Supplement* and the *Federal Reporter*, books that publish the cases decided by federal courts.

Georgia is in the Eleventh Circuit. Therefore, cases from the U.S. District Court for the three districts of Georgia are appealed to the U.S. Court of Appeals for the Eleventh Circuit. This circuit encompasses Georgia, Florida, and Alabama. Prior to the creation of the Eleventh Circuit on October 1, 1981, Georgia was in the Fifth Circuit.

The highest court in the federal system is the United States Supreme Court. It decides cases concerning the United States Constitution and federal statutes. This court does not have the final say on matters of purely state law; that authority rests with the highest court of each state. Parties who wish to have the U.S. Supreme Court hear their case must file a petition for *certiorari*, as the court has discretion over which cases it hears.

The federal judiciary website at www.uscourts.gov contains maps, court addresses, explanations of jurisdiction, and other helpful information.

C. Courts of Other States

Not all states have the three-tier court system of Georgia and the federal judiciary. Another difference in some court systems is that the "supreme" court is not the highest court. In New York, the trial courts are called supreme courts and the highest court is the Court of Appeals. Two other states, Massachusetts and Maine, call their highest courts the Supreme Judicial Court.

Citation manuals are good references for learning the names and hierarchy of the courts, as well as for learning proper citation to legal authorities. The two most popular are *The Bluebook: A Uniform System of Citation*, written by students from several law schools,[8] and the *ALWD Citation Manual: A Professional System of Citation*, written by Dean Darby Dickerson and the Association of Legal Writing Directors.[9]

V. Overview of the Research Process

Conducting effective legal research means following a process. This process leads to the authority that controls a legal issue as well as to commentary that may help you analyze new and complex legal matters. The outline in Table 1-2 presents the basic research process.

This basic process should be customized for each research project. Consider whether you need to follow all eight steps, and if so, in what order. If you are unfamiliar with an area of law, you should follow each step of the process in the order indicated. Beginning with secondary sources will provide both context for the issues you must research and citations to relevant primary authority. As you gain experience in researching legal questions, you may choose to modify the process. For example, if you know that a situation is controlled by a statute, you may choose to begin with that step.

---

8. *The Bluebook: A Uniform System of Citation* (Columbia Law Review Ass'n et al. eds., 18th ed. 2005). This book uses the *Bluebook*'s system of citation for practitioners.

9. Association of Legal Writing Directors & Darby Dickerson, *ALWD Citation Manual: A Professional System of Citation* (3d ed. 2006).

Table 1-2. Overview of the Research Process

Step 1   Generate a list of *research terms*.

Step 2   Determine whether the issue is controlled by *state law, federal law*, or *both*.

Step 3   Consult *secondary sources* and practice aids, including treatises, legal encyclopedias, *American Law Reports*, and law review articles. These sources provide helpful background information and point to primary authority. Remember, many secondary sources are available in print and online.

Step 4   Find controlling *constitutional provisions, statutes*, or *rules*. In print, review indexes for your research terms, then read the relevant sections. Online, search the appropriate table of contents or conduct a full-text search. Most databases have a useful table of contents.

Step 5   Use *online tools* or *digests* to find citations to cases. A digest is essentially a multi-volume topic index of cases in a certain jurisdiction or subject area.

Step 6   Read the cases either online or in *reporters*. A reporter series publishes the full text of cases in a certain jurisdiction or subject area.

Step 7   *Update* by using a citator to ensure your legal authorities have not been repealed, reversed, modified, or otherwise changed. Use online citators for the most current information.

Step 8   *Outline* your legal analysis based on your research. You are finished researching when there are no holes left in your analysis and when research in various resources leads to the same authorities.

A. Generating Research Terms

Many legal resources in print use lengthy indexes as the starting point for finding legal authority. Electronic sources often require the researcher to enter words that are likely to appear in a synopsis or in the full text of relevant documents. To ensure you are thorough in beginning a research project, you will need a comprehensive list of words, terms, and phrases that may lead to law on point. These may be legal terms or common words that describe the client's situation. The items on this list are *research terms*.

Organized brainstorming is the best way to compile a comprehensive list of research terms. First, think of the *parties* involved in the problem, along with the *places* and *things* involved in the problem. Also, consider the potential *claims* and *defenses*, along with the *relief sought*.[10] Generate a broad range of research terms regarding the facts, issues, and desired solutions of your client's situation. Include in the list both specific and general words. Try to think of synonyms and antonyms for each term since at this point you are uncertain which terms an index or database may include. Using a legal dictionary or thesaurus may generate additional terms.

As an example of how you might use these categories to generate research terms, assume you have been asked to research the following situation. A patron was at a car wash facility, and, when he stepped out of his car to pay the attendant, he fell on "slick ice." The patron was injured. It was the patron's first visit to the car wash. He believed that the car wash attendant knew about the icy condition of the premises, but did nothing to warn him or remedy it. Table 1-3 lists possible research terms, using the categories discussed above.

As your research progresses, you will learn new research terms to include in the list and decide to take others off. For example, you may read cases that give you insights into the key words judges tend to use in discussing this topic. Alternatively, you may learn a "term of art," a word or phrase that has special meaning in a particular area of law. These need to be added to the list.

B. Researching the Law — Organization of This Text

The remainder of this book explains how to use your research terms to conduct legal research in a variety of sources. Although the research process often begins with secondary sources, this book begins with primary authority because locating that authority is the goal

---

10. Amy E. Sloan, *Basic Legal Research: Tools and Strategies* 23–25 (3d ed. 2005).

Table 1-3. Research Terms

Parties:	car wash attendant owner of the business patron
Places and things:	car wash ice Georgia
Potential claims and defenses:	negligence car wash as nuisance strict liability assumption of the risk contributory negligence
Relief:	compensation for personal injuries

of research. Chapter 2 addresses the Georgia judicial opinions and reporters. Chapter 3 discusses using digests and online sources to research judicial decisions. Chapter 4 focuses on statutory research, constitutional research, and court rules. Chapter 5 addresses legislative history research, and Chapter 6 addresses administrative law.

After this focus on various authorities, the following chapters explain how to update legal authority using citators in Chapter 7 and how to use secondary sources in Chapter 8. Chapter 9 discusses legal ethics research.

Chapter 10 delves into the advantages and disadvantages of online research and provides basic information for conducting legal research online. Although we provide online sources throughout the text, this chapter provides additional information.

Chapter 11 discusses research strategies as well as organizational skills for your research. You may prefer to skim that chapter now and refer to it frequently, even though a number of references in it will not become clear until you have read the intervening chapters.

Appendix A provides an overview of the conventions lawyers follow in citing legal authority in their documents. Appendix B is a selected bibliography of research guides and texts on legal analysis. Appendix C is a subject bibliography of Georgia practice materials.

Chapter 2

Judicial Opinions and Reporters

After reading this chapter you will be able to:
- recognize and use the information in a case citation;
- identify the various parts of a case;
- know the different reporters for Georgia cases; and
- recognize the reporters for federal cases.

I. Judicial Opinions — General Information

A judicial opinion, also called a case, is written by a court to explain its decision in a particular dispute. Cases are published in rough chronological order in books called *reporters*. Some reporters include only cases decided by a certain court; for example, the *Georgia Reports* publishes only cases decided by the Supreme Court of Georgia. Other reporters include cases from courts within a specific geographic region; for example, the *South Eastern Reporter* publishes the cases reported in the southeastern United States. Still other reporters publish only those cases that deal with a certain topic, such as bankruptcy or education. Even when cases are available in electronic format, they are often retrieved by reference to their print reporters.

A. Deciphering a Case Citation

Cases are typically located through their citations. In a case citation, the title of the reporter is abbreviated. All of the reporters have

Table 2-1. A Typical Case Citation

Case Name	Volume Number	Official Reporter	Page Number	Volume Number	Regional Reporter	Page Number	Year Decided
Rector v. Rector	244	Ga.	315	260	S.E.2d	55	1979

standard abbreviations. For example, S.E.2d is the abbreviation for *South Eastern Reporter, Second Series.*

You can easily decipher a citation abbreviation by checking *The Bluebook: A Uniform System of Citation* or the *ALWD Citation Manual: A Professional System of Citation.* A typical citation includes components as illustrated in Table 2-1. In a legal document, the citation would be written *Rector v. Rector,* 244 Ga. 315, 260 S.E.2d 55 (1979).

B. Official and Unofficial Reporters

There is a distinction in case reporting between official and unofficial reporters. Official reporters are simply those reporters that a statute or a court order designates as official. For example, *Georgia Reports* and *Georgia Appeals Reports* are official reporters. An example of an unofficial reporter is the *South Eastern Reporter* published by Thomson/West (hereinafter West).

The text of an opinion as it is published in an unofficial reporter is the same as the text of the opinion as it is published in the official reporter; however, unofficial reporters include editorial enhancements, such as headnotes, topics, and key numbers, as aids to researchers.

C. Parallel Case Citations

A citation to the same case published in a different reporter is a *parallel citation.* Parallel citations are different citations to the same case in official versus unofficial reporters.

There are several ways to find a parallel citation if the researcher only knows one citation. To expedite the search for a parallel citation, a case printed in a bound official reporter (e.g., *Georgia Reports* or *Georgia Appeals Reports*) or in a West reporter includes the parallel citation. West publishes alternative sources, including the *Georgia Blue and White Book* and the *National Reporter Blue Book*, which list conversion tables for parallel citations. The researcher can also find parallel citations by using either Shepard's or KeyCite. Both Shepard's and KeyCite are explained in Chapter 7.

D. Local Citation Rules for Georgia

Appendix A of this book includes a thorough discussion of citing documents correctly. For documents submitted to the Georgia courts, you should cite to the source or sources required by local rules.[1] According to the Georgia Supreme Court Rules, citations must include the volume and page number of the official Georgia reporters.[2] A researcher should cite unreported cases by referring to the Supreme Court or Court of Appeals case number and date of decision.[3] To ensure that all researchers can locate a case by official citation or regional reporter citation, researchers should include the parallel citations.[4] An example of a parallel citation is *Ponder v. Williams*, 80 Ga. App. 145, 55 S.E.2d 668 (1949).

When writing a memorandum or brief for submission to a state court in Georgia and citing a case from outside Georgia, such as North Carolina, researchers should cite only the regional reporter with the court identification in parentheses, for example, *Woodson v. Bowland*, 407 S.E.2d 222 (N.C. 1991). For case citations in other forms of legal writing, such as law review articles and legal memoranda, researchers should cite only the appropriate regional re-

---

1. *The Bluebook*, B5.1.3 at 8, Table BT.2 at 27, and *ALWD* at 7–8, App. 2 at 415.
2. Ga. Sup. Ct. R. 22; Ga. Ct. App. R. 24(d).
3. Ga. Ct. App. R. 24(d).
4. *The Bluebook*, Rule 10.3.1 at 86–87.

porter, for example, *Brannon v. Brannon*, 407 S.E.2d 748 (Ga. 1991).[5]

II. Reporters for Georgia Cases

A. *Georgia Reports* and *Georgia Appeals Reports*

Since the Georgia legislature directs the publication of the judicial opinions under the *Official Code of Georgia Annotated* (O.C.G.A.) § 50-18-20 (2002), *Georgia Reports* and *Georgia Appeals Reports* are designated the state's "official" case law reporters. As of July 2004, the Supreme Court of Georgia designated LexisNexis the publisher of *Georgia Reports* and *Georgia Appeals Reports*. The indexes and research tables contained in each volume are the product of the legal editorial staff of the publisher.

Georgia Reports includes all Georgia Supreme Court decisions since 1846. *Georgia Appeals Reports* contains most of the Court of Appeals decisions since 1907. The Georgia Court of Appeals Rules dictate the publication of opinions for that court.[6] Judges sometimes vote not to publish a decision if it does not set precedent. When an opinion is not published, there is a list showing the author of the opinion and those who concurred. Unreported opinions are not binding precedent of the court.[7] However, such opinions establish the law of the particular case.[8]

Both *Georgia Reports* and *Georgia Appeals Reports* include the texts of the opinions without any synopses or headnotes, which limits a researcher to the text of the opinion without editorial assistance. Although there are no headnotes (one-paragraph summaries of the major issues) for cases, each legal issue is numbered within the actual text of the opinion.

---

5. *Id.* at 87.
6. Ga. Ct. App. R. 34.
7. Ga. Ct. App. R. 33(b).
8. O.C.G.A. § 9-11-60(h) (2002).

Georgia Reports and *Georgia Appeals Reports* organize cases by the date of the decision and provide the parallel citation to the *South Eastern Reporter.* Each volume includes a Table of Case Names and a Topical Index.

Both of the official reporters share the same weekly advance sheet service, titled *Georgia Advance Sheets.* Advance sheets to any reporter are weekly paperbacks of new opinions. The volume and pagination of the advance sheets are identical to the hardbound *Georgia Reports* and *Georgia Appeals Reports.* Although the advance sheets are published weekly, the cases are one to two months old. Certiorari Tables, also included in the advance sheets, list the applications to the Georgia Supreme Court for writ of certiorari. Each advance sheet also includes useful research information, including indexes, parallel tables, and new court rules.

B. *South Eastern Reporter*

Since 1887, the *South Eastern Reporter,* published by West, has printed opinions of the Georgia Supreme Court and the Georgia Court of Appeals. The reporter included only the Georgia Supreme Court opinions from 1887 to 1907, but the reporter has included Georgia Court of Appeals decisions since 1907. In addition to Georgia cases, the *South Eastern Reporter* includes appellate decisions from North Carolina, South Carolina, Virginia, and West Virginia. West's regional reporters are a set of reporters that divides the fifty states and the District of Columbia into seven national regions: Atlantic, North Eastern, North Western, Pacific, South Eastern, South Western, and Southern. The coverage of each regional reporter is not the same as the composition of the federal circuits. Table 2-2 exemplifies this. For example, the Eleventh Circuit is comprised of Alabama, Florida, and Georgia. However, Alabama and Florida cases are reported in the *Southern Reporter* and Georgia cases are reported in the *South Eastern Reporter.*

The regional reporters cover the opinions of state courts of last resort and intermediate appellate courts (in states that have such courts). Often, when a reporter reaches a certain volume number, the publisher begins another series. In 1939, after volume 200 of *South Eastern Reporter* was published, the publisher decided to begin again with volume

1 of *South Eastern Reporter, Second Series.* To find a case in a reporter with multiple series, you must know which series to consult.

Several tables first appear in the advance sheets of the *South Eastern Reporter* and later in the bound volume, including Certiorari Tables and the Key Number Digest. Researchers most frequently use the Table of Cases Reported, where cases are listed by both plaintiff and defendant. Although the advance sheets are weekly, the cases are one to two months old.

Table 2-2. States Included in West's Regional Reporters with Corresponding Federal Judicial Circuit Number

State	State Cases Available in West's Regional Reporters	Federal Judicial Circuit
Alabama	*Southern Reporter*	11th Circuit
Alaska	*Pacific Reporter*	9th Circuit
Arizona	*Pacific Reporter*	9th Circuit
Arkansas	*South Western Reporter*	8th Circuit
California	*Pacific Reporter*	9th Circuit
Colorado	*Pacific Reporter*	10th Circuit
Connecticut	*Atlantic Reporter*	2d Circuit
Delaware	*Atlantic Reporter*	3d Circuit
District of Columbia	*Atlantic Reporter*	D.C. Circuit, Federal Circuit
Florida	*Southern Reporter*	11th Circuit
Georgia	*South Eastern Reporter*	11th Circuit
Hawaii	*Pacific Reporter*	9th Circuit
Idaho	*Pacific Reporter*	9th Circuit
Illinois	*North Eastern Reporter*	7th Circuit
Indiana	*North Eastern Reporter*	7th Circuit
Iowa	*North Western Reporter*	8th Circuit
Kansas	*Pacific Reporter*	10th Circuit
Kentucky	*South Western Reporter*	6th Circuit
Louisiana	*Southern Reporter*	5th Circuit
Maine	*Atlantic Reporter*	1st Circuit
Maryland	*Atlantic Reporter*	4th Circuit
Massachusetts	*North Eastern Reporter*	1st Circuit
Michigan	*North Western Reporter*	6th Circuit
Minnesota	*North Western Reporter*	8th Circuit
Mississippi	*Southern Reporter*	5th Circuit
Missouri	*South Western Reporter*	8th Circuit

Table 2-2. States Included in West's Regional Reporters, cont'd with Corresponding Federal Judicial Circuit Number

State	State Cases Available in West's Regional Reporters	Federal Judicial Circuit
Montana	*Pacific Reporter*	9th Circuit
Nebraska	*North Western Reporter*	8th Circuit
Nevada	*Pacific Reporter*	9th Circuit
New Hampshire	*Atlantic Reporter*	1st Circuit
New Jersey	*Atlantic Reporter*	3d Circuit
New Mexico	*Pacific Reporter*	10th Circuit
New York	*North Eastern Reporter*	2d Circuit
North Carolina	*South Eastern Reporter*	4th Circuit
North Dakota	*North Western Reporter*	8th Circuit
Ohio	*North Eastern Reporter*	6th Circuit
Oklahoma	*Pacific Reporter*	10th Circuit
Oregon	*Pacific Reporter*	9th Circuit
Pennsylvania	*Atlantic Reporter*	3d Circuit
Rhode Island	*Atlantic Reporter*	1st Circuit
South Carolina	*South Eastern Reporter*	4th Circuit
South Dakota	*North Western Reporter*	8th Circuit
Tennessee	*South Western Reporter*	6th Circuit
Texas	*South Western Reporter*	5th Circuit
Utah	*Pacific Reporter*	10th Circuit
Vermont	*Atlantic Reporter*	2d Circuit
Virginia	*South Eastern Reporter*	4th Circuit
Washington	*Pacific Reporter*	9th Circuit
West Virginia	*South Eastern Reporter*	4th Circuit
Wisconsin	*North Western Reporter*	7th Circuit
Wyoming	*Pacific Reporter*	10th Circuit

C. *Georgia Cases*

Georgia Cases, published by West since 1939, is a compilation of Georgia cases reprinted from the pages of the *South Eastern Reporter 2d*. It retains the same volume and pagination as the *South Eastern Reporter 2d*; cases from other states are simply omitted. For those lawyers who concentrate on Georgia law, *Georgia Cases* is a very convenient source for printed cases. Table 2-3 provides the names of the reporters that include Georgia cases.

Table 2-3. Reporters for Georgia Cases

Court Deciding the Case	Reporter Name	Abbreviation(s)
Supreme Court of Georgia	*Georgia Reports* (official) *South Eastern Reporter*	Ga. S.E. or S.E.2d
Court of Appeals of Georgia	*Georgia Appeals Reports* (official) *South Eastern Reporter*	Ga. App. S.E. or S.E.2d
Lower Georgia courts	Selective reporting. See Section III.C of this chapter.	

D. Georgia Supreme Court Briefs

Briefs and petitions submitted to the Georgia Supreme Court from 1990 to the present are available on Westlaw. Briefs and motions from a variety of Georgia state cases from 2000 to the present are available on LexisNexis.

III. Reading Cases and Locating Current Cases

A. Parts of a Reported Case

Understanding the structure of a case will help you analyze cases more effectively. Table 2-4 demonstrates how the components explained below appear on the first pages of an actual case in an unofficial reporter.

Case Name. The name of a case includes the names of the parties. Most cases are named for the parties involved to indicate who is suing whom, e.g., *Brannon v. Brannon*. Some cases may have only one name with a Latin phrase attached, e.g., *In re Seiferth*. In a criminal case, since the state brings the action, the first party will often be the state itself, e.g., *State v. Birditt*.

When a case begins in the trial court, the first name is the plaintiff, or the party suing, and the name after the "v." is the defendant. On appeal, the name of the petitioner or appellant will be listed first; the name of the respondent or appellee will be listed second. Therefore, if the defendant in the trial court brings an appeal, his or her name may be listed first in the appellate case.

When you read a case in a print reporter or online, you will often find several plaintiffs, defendants, or cross-complainants. Correct citation form requires that only the first-named plaintiff and the first-named defendant be listed.

The case name that appears at the top of the page in the reporters is not in correct citation format and should not be followed as an example of *Bluebook* or *ALWD Citation Manual* format.

Docket Number. When a case is filed with the court clerk, it is assigned a *docket number* that remains with the case and is used to keep track of documents filed in the course of the litigation. In Georgia, the Supreme Court uses a case numbering system that identifies both the year that a case is calendared and what type of appeal it represents. For instance, the case S03A1258 was on direct appeal to the Supreme Court (hence the letter "S"). It was submitted to the Court for decision during 2003. The "A" signifies it was on appeal; the numbers at the end are the file number. The Supreme Court website at www.gasupreme.us/computer_docket.php lists the letter designations used by the Court to identify the various types of appeals brought before the Court. In contrast, Georgia Court of Appeals dockets begin with "A," e.g., No. A05A2138.

Date. A case will include the exact month, day, and year that it was decided. For citation purposes, use only the year the case was decided.

Synopsis. Attorney-editors at West write a synopsis or brief description of each case. Currently, the synopsis is broken into two categories: background and holding. The synopsis also includes the name of the judge writing the opinion. If you have many cases to read, you can quickly scan the synopses to weed out the irrelevant cases, but be advised that the synopsis is not part of the opinion. Moreover, you must never cite the synopsis, even when it gives an excellent summary of the case, since it is not authoritative. At the end of the synopsis, you will find the disposition of the case. The disposition of the case is the court's decision to affirm, reverse, remand, or vacate the decision.

Headnotes, Topics, and Key Numbers. Court decisions contain at least one legal issue. An issue is the question raised when the facts of the case intersect with the rules of law. West attorney-editors identify the legal issues in the cases and discuss each issue in a *headnote.* Each headnote is usually one sentence. In reporters, headnotes appear between the synopsis and the opinion. A headnote in a reporter begins with a number in boldface type followed by a topic name and key number.

Headnotes are numbered, so you can use them as you would a table of contents to the case. Numbers corresponding to the headnote numbers appear inside brackets within the text of the opinion. The bracketed number indicates the portion of the text summarized by a particular headnote.

Immediately following the headnote number is the broad legal topic under which a West attorney-editor has classified that particular headnote. *Topics* are the main headnote classification.

After the topic in a West reporter, a key number is given. The *key number* represents a specific aspect or subsection of a topic.

Headnotes from cases are grouped in books called *digests,* where they are arranged by topics and key numbers. Once you find a relevant topic and key number, you may use the topic and key number in the *Georgia Digest,* the *South Eastern Digest,* or any other West digest to search for additional cases on the same topic. The lines of text in the digest are actually the headnotes themselves.

Attorneys. Immediately preceding the text of the opinion, you will find the names of the attorneys of record, along with the names of the attorneys' firms.

Opinion. The actual text of the decision in a case is called the *opinion.* The structure of an opinion generally includes a description of the nature of the case, a statement of the issues presented, the facts, the errors assigned if the case is on appeal, and the disposition.

If the judges who heard an appellate case do not agree on the outcome or the reasons for the outcome, there may be several opinions. The opinion supported by a majority of the judges is called the *majority* opinion. In Georgia, there are *per curiam* opinions. *Per curiam* means "by the court." That phrase distinguishes an opinion of the whole court from an opinion written by any one judge. An opinion written to agree with the outcome but not the reasoning of the majority is called a *concurring* opinion. A dissenting judge disagrees with the opinion and judgment of the majority and writes a *dissenting* opinion. While only the majority opinion is binding precedent, the other opinions provide valuable insights and may be cited as persuasive authority.

Table 2-4. Parts of a Case

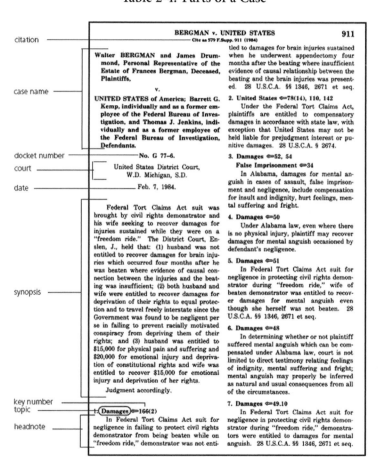

Reprinted from the *Federal Supplement* with permission of Thomson/West.

B. Current Case Law and Online Sources of Cases

Once a case is issued by the court, it is gathered with other opinions into softbound weekly advance sheets. Opinions in the advance sheets are arranged chronologically. Advance sheets provide subject indexes and an alphabetical list of cases.

Although the official and unofficial advance sheets are published weekly, it still takes several months for an opinion to appear in print. The *Daily Report*'s Opinions Weekly in the *Daily Report* (formerly *Fulton County Daily Report*) comes out before the advance sheets and includes the opinions of the Supreme Court and the Court of Appeals. LexisNexis provides access to the *Daily Report* editions from 1996 to the present; Westlaw's coverage begins in 1998.

Table 2-5 includes online sources for Georgia case law. An expanded table appears in the appendix to this chapter.

C. Trial Level Reporters

Georgia reporters do not report trial level cases. However, since 1988, the *Georgia Trial Reporter*, available in print and online at www.juryverdicts.com, has published a monthly summary of all available superior and state court civil jury trials in the Atlanta met-

Table 2-5. Online Sources of Georgia Cases

Source Name	Web Address	Commercial/Free
Casemaker	www.gabar.org/ casemaker	Free to Georgia Bar members
Court of Appeals of Georgia	www.gaappeals.us	Free (includes last five years of cases)
Supreme Court of Georgia	www.gasupreme.us	Free (2004–present)
LexisNexis	www.lexis.com	Commercial
Loislaw	www.loislaw.com	Commercial
Westlaw	www.westlaw.com	Commercial

ropolitan area that result in a verdict. Although a researcher cannot cite these opinions, the information is particularly valuable for verdicts. Forty jury cases appear each month, along with eight indexes, allowing quick access to experts, injuries, subject matter, attorneys, defendants, jurisdiction, judge, and insurance carrier. Additionally, since December 2005, West has published significant trial court decisions in *West's Jury Verdicts Georgia Reports*, available in print and on Westlaw.

IV. Reporters for Federal Cases

So far, this chapter has dealt with reporters for Georgia cases. This part explains the reporters for cases decided by federal courts. Table 2-6 lists the federal court reporters, along with their citation abbreviations.

A. U.S. Supreme Court

At the apex of the federal judicial pyramid is the U.S. Supreme Court. Almost all of its business consists of reviewing the judgments of lower courts. These may be the decisions of lower federal courts (the federal circuit courts of appeals and the federal district courts) or judgments of state courts of last resort that deal with questions of federal law.

Table 2-6. Reporters for Federal Court Cases

Court Deciding the Case	Reporter Name	Abbreviation(s)
U.S. Supreme Court	*United States Reports* (official) *Supreme Court Reporter* *United States Supreme Court Reports, Lawyers' Edition*	U.S. S. Ct. L. Ed. or L. Ed. 2d
U.S. Courts of Appeals	*Federal Reporter*	F., F.2d, or F.3d
U.S. District Courts	*Federal Supplement*	F. Supp. or F. Supp. 2d

If a federal question arises in state litigation, the parties must pursue that question on appeal up through the state court system before the case is eligible for review by the U.S. Supreme Court. Generally, the Supreme Court hears only cases already appealed to a state's highest appellate court or to one of the thirteen federal circuit courts of appeals.

The U.S. Supreme Court could not possibly hear all of the cases that come before it. It disposes of most appeals summarily by denying petitions for a writ of certiorari. This is a device used by the Supreme Court in choosing the cases it wishes to hear during a session.

Decisions of the U.S. Supreme Court are reported in three reporters: *United States Reports*, which is the official reporter; *Supreme Court Reporter*, which is a West publication; and *United States Supreme Court Reports, Lawyers' Edition*, another unofficial reporter, published by LexisNexis, now in its second series. Although *United States Reports* is the official reporter, meaning that you should cite it if possible, that series frequently publishes cases several years after they are decided. Even the advance sheets can run several years late. Thus, for recent cases, you will often cite the *Supreme Court Reporter*. Another source for finding recent cases from the Supreme Court is *United States Law Week*, published by the Bureau of National Affairs. This service publishes the full text of cases from the Supreme Court and provides summaries of important decisions of state and federal courts.

There are a number of online sources for U.S. Supreme Court opinions. The Court's website at www.supremecourtus.gov/opinions/opinions.html includes opinions within hours. An educational site supported by Cornell University at www.law.cornell.edu/supct/index.html also provides decisions quickly.

B. Jurisdiction of U.S. Courts of Appeals and West's *Federal Reporter*

Below the U.S. Supreme Court in the federal system are thirteen federal courts of appeals and numerous federal district courts. The jurisdiction of the federal courts of appeals (often referred to as circuit courts) consists of appeals from decisions of district courts, together with appeals from decisions of federal administrative agencies (e.g., the Federal Communications Commission).

Since 1880, the decisions of the federal courts of appeals have been published in West's *Federal Reporter*, now in its third series. The abbreviations for these reporters are F., F.2d, and F.3d. Table 2-2 lists each state and its corresponding federal judicial circuit.

C. Jurisdiction of U.S. District Courts and West's *Federal Supplement*

The jurisdiction of the district courts is the most complex part of federal jurisdiction. A case will be tried in a district court if it "arises under" federal law for purposes of federal trial court jurisdiction. Federal district courts also have jurisdiction over civil cases involving parties from different states; these are known as diversity cases. The criminal jurisdiction of the district courts includes all prosecutions for federal crimes.

Since 1932, the decisions of the federal district courts have been published in West's *Federal Supplement* series of reporters. Selected cases from the U.S. District Courts, the federal trial courts, are reported in *Federal Supplement* and *Federal Supplement 2d*. The citation abbreviations for these reporters are F. Supp. and F. Supp. 2d. Some opinions are available on the federal judiciary and Cornell websites as well. A very high percentage of federal district court opinions are not reported; however, they are available on LexisNexis and Westlaw.

D. Special Courts and Reporters

A few special federal courts, such as the U.S. Tax Court, publish their own decisions. West publishes the *Bankruptcy Reporter*, which includes cases from the federal bankruptcy courts plus district court bankruptcy cases not reported in the *Federal Supplement*. It also publishes *Federal Rules Decisions*, which includes federal district court cases that analyze federal rules of civil and criminal procedure.

V. Unreported Opinions

You may be surprised to learn that the great majority of federal and some state judicial opinions are not reported at all. Sometimes an opinion is not reported because the court deems it redundant of previous decisions; other opinions are not reported because they are determined to lack precedential value. Court rules in each jurisdiction indicate when reporting of an opinion is necessary or desirable, and the rules vary among jurisdictions. Nearly all the decisions of courts of last resort within the state and federal system are reported in full.

Most state trial-level cases are not reported. In fact, most trial court actions do not produce a written opinion at all. Trial transcripts and documents filed with the clerk of court make up a record of the action. These materials may be available as public records, but they are rarely published.

A very high percentage of federal district court opinions are not reported. In fact, not all federal appellate cases are reported. The trend has been to report fewer opinions on a percentage basis. Because the absolute number of cases being decided continues to rise, a large number of opinions are reported.

Many opinions not designated for inclusion in the reporters are nevertheless available online. There has been much debate in legal circles as to whether unreported opinions can serve as precedent, that is, whether they can be cited as authority. Some jurisdictions permit citation of unreported opinions, while others permit citation only in limited circumstances or prohibit it entirely. In April 2006, the U.S. Supreme Court adopted Federal Rule of Appellate Procedure 32.1, which provides that unpublished federal judicial opinions, orders, judgments, or other written dispositions issued on or after January 1, 2007, may be cited in the federal courts. The courts are free to decide the precedential weight of the unpublished decisions, but they may not prohibit their citation.

Even when they have no or limited precedential authority, unreported opinions can help you understand an issue and determine judicial thinking. For example, if you are going before Judge Smith in a products liability case, it may be valuable to know what Judge Smith has done before in similar cases. It may also be useful to know which parties have been involved in prior litigation and what arguments were considered. Thus, unreported cases have many uses.

VI. Reading and Analyzing Cases

Once you locate a case, you must read it, understand it, and analyze its potential relevance to the problem you are researching. An attorney, judge, or client who has asked you to do the research will not be satisfied if you return from the library with a stack of photocopied cases you have not yet analyzed.

Do not expect reading a case to be easy. Understanding a case may take more mental work than you have ever dedicated to a few pages. It is not unusual for beginning lawyers to read complex cases at around just a few pages per hour. Often this reading is interrupted by referring to a law dictionary to try to understand the terms used. Early efforts will be more productive if you have a basic understanding of civil procedure terms and the fundamental aspects of case analysis, and then follow the strategies outlined at the end of this chapter.

A. Thimbleful of Civil Procedure

The person who believes he was harmed begins civil litigation by filing a *complaint* in the court he selects. The *plaintiff* is the person who files the complaint; the person against whom the complaint is filed is the *defendant*. The complaint names the parties, states the facts, notes the relevant laws, and asks for relief. Courts vary considerably in how much information is required at this stage of the litigation. In general, the complaint must be specific enough to put the defendant on notice of the legal concerns at issue and to allow her to prepare a defense.

The defendant has a limited amount of time in which to file a response to this complaint. (If the defendant does nothing within the prescribed time, the plaintiff can ask the court for a *default judgment*, which would grant the plaintiff the relief sought in the complaint.) One form of response to the complaint is an *answer*. In the answer, the defendant admits to the parts of the complaint that she knows are true, denies those things that she disputes, and asserts no knowledge of other allegations. The defendant also may raise affirmative defenses.

Throughout the litigation, parties submit a variety of papers to the court for its consideration. Some require no action or response from the court, for example, the filing of the complaint. In other instances, a party asks the court to make a decision or take action. An example is a motion for *summary judgment*, where a party asks the court to decide in that party's favor without the need for a trial.

When the trial judge grants a motion that ends a case, the losing party can appeal. The appealing party is called the *appellant*; the other party is the *respondent*. In deciding an appeal from an order granting a motion, the appellate court is deciding whether the trial judge was correct in issuing the order at that stage of the litigation. If the appellate court agrees with the decision of the trial judge, it will *affirm*. If not, the court will *reverse* the order granting the motion and in some instances *remand* the case back to the trial court.

Even at trial, the parties might make motions that can be appealed. For example, during the trial, the plaintiff presents his evidence first. After all of the plaintiff's witnesses have testified, the defendant may move for a *judgment as a matter of law*, arguing that the plaintiff cannot win based on the evidence presented and asking for an immediate decision. An order granting that motion could be appealed.

Most of the reported cases are appeals of orders granting motions. These cases apply different standards of review, depending on the motion that is the object of the appeal. While standards of review are beyond the scope of this book, understanding the procedural posture of the case is crucial to understanding the court's holding. The relevant rules of civil procedure will guide your analysis. Texts listed in Appendix B of this book contain helpful explanations as well.

B. Analyzing the Substance of Cases

Early in your career, it may be difficult to determine whether a case is relevant to your research problem. If the case concerns the same legally significant facts as your client's situation and the court applies law on point for your problem, then the case is relevant. Legally significant facts are those that affect the court's decision. Some attorneys call these outcome-determinative facts or key facts. Which facts are legally significant depends on the case. The height of the defendant in a contract dispute is unlikely to be legally significant, but that fact may be critical in a criminal case where the only eyewitness testified that the thief was about five feet tall.

Rarely will your research reveal a case with facts that are exactly the same as your client's situation. Rather, several cases may involve facts that are similar to your client's situation but not exactly the same. Your job is to determine whether the facts are similar enough for a court to apply the law in the same way and reach the same outcome. If the court reached a decision favorable to your client, you will highlight the similarities. If, on the other hand, the court reached an unfavorable decision from your client's perspective, you may argue that the case is distinguishable from yours based on its facts or that its reasoning is faulty. You have an ethical duty to ensure that the court knows about a case directly on point, even if the outcome of that case is adverse to your client.

You are also unlikely to find one case that addresses all aspects of your client's situation. Most legal claims have several elements or factors. *Elements* are required subparts of a claim, while *factors* are important aspects but not required. If a court decides that one element is not met, it may not discuss others. In a different case, the court may decide that two factors are so overwhelming that others have no impact on the outcome. In these circumstances, you would have to find other cases that analyze the other elements or factors.

Once you determine that a case is relevant to some portion of your analysis, you must decide how heavily it will weigh in your analysis. Two important points need to be considered here. One is the concept of *stare decisis*; the other is the difference between the holding of the case and dicta within that case.

Stare decisis means "to stand by things decided." This means that courts must follow prior opinions, ensuring consistency in the application of the law. This requirement, however, is limited to the courts within one jurisdiction. The Court of Appeals of Georgia must follow the decisions of the Georgia Supreme Court, but not those of the courts of any other state. The concept of *stare decisis* also refers to a court with respect to its own opinions. The Court of Appeals, thus, should follow its own earlier cases in deciding new matters. If a court decides not to continue following its earlier cases, it is usually because of changes in society that have outdated the law of the earlier case, or because a new statute has been enacted that changes the legal landscape.

Under *stare decisis,* courts are required to follow the holding of prior cases. The *holding* is the court's ultimate decision on the matter of law at issue in the case. Other statements or observations included in the opinion are not binding; they are referred to as *dicta.* For example, a court in a property dispute may hold that the land belongs to X. In reaching that decision, the court may note that had the facts been slightly different, it would have decided the land belonged to Y. That observation is not binding on future courts, though it may be cited as persuasive authority.

After finding a number of cases that have similar facts, that discuss the same legal issue, and that are binding on your client, the next step is to synthesize the cases to state and explain the legal rule. Sometimes a court states the rule fully; if not, piece together the information from the relevant cases to state the rule completely but concisely. Then use the analysis and facts of various cases to explain the law. Decide how the rule applies to the client's facts, and determine your conclusion. Note that this method of synthesis is much more than mere summaries of all the various cases. Legal analysis texts referenced in Appendix B of this book explain synthesis in detail.

C. Strategies for Reading Cases

The following strategies may help you understand cases more quickly and more thoroughly.

Review the synopsis quickly to determine whether the case seems to be on point. If so, skim the headnotes to find the particular portion of the case that is relevant. Remember that one case may discuss several issues of law, only one or two of which may interest you. Go to the portion of the case identified by the relevant headnote and decide whether it is important for your project.

If so, skim the entire case to get a feeling for what happened and why, focusing on the portion of the case identified by the relevant headnote.

Read the case slowly and carefully. Skip the parts that are obviously not pertinent to your problem. For example, if you are researching a property question, there is no need to scrutinize the tort issue that is not pertinent to your property question.

At the end of each paragraph or page, consider what you have read. If you cannot summarize it, try reading the material again.

The next time you read the case, take notes. The notes may be in the form of a formal "case brief," or they may be scribbles that only you can understand. Regardless of the form, the process of taking notes will help you parse through, identify, and comprehend the essential concepts of the case. In law school, the notes will record your understanding of the case both for class discussion and for the end of the semester when you begin to review for exams. When preparing to write a legal document, the notes will assist you in organizing your analysis into an outline.

Note that skimming text online or highlighting a printed page is often not sufficient to achieve thorough comprehension of judicial opinions.

The following appendix lists the free and commercial sources of
Georgia cases online.

Appendix 2-A. Online Sources for Georgia Cases

Casemaker www.gabar.org/casemaker *Free to members of the* *State Bar of Georgia*	Content:	Supreme Court cases (1939–present) Court of Appeals cases (1939–present)
	Update:	Supreme Court (within 48 hours of posting) Court of Appeals (within 72 hours of receipt from court)
Georgia Court of Appeals www.gaappeals.us *Free*	Content:	Court of Appeals cases (most recent five years) (click on "Opinions" and register on LexisOne) Status of Court of Appeals cases (since January 2003) (click on "Docket/Case Search")
	Update:	Continuously
	Notes:	Search by keyword; no browsing options
Georgia Supreme Court www.gasupreme.us *Free*	Content:	Supreme Court cases in PDF (last two years) Certiorari granted and docket information also available
	Update:	Weekly
	Notes:	Arranged chronologically; search by docket number or case name
LexisNexis www.lexis.com *Commercial*	Content:	Supreme Court cases (1846–present) Court of Appeals cases (1907–present) Briefs from selected Georgia cases (2000–present)
	Update:	As received from the court; usually 24–48 hours
Loislaw www.loislaw.com *Commercial*	Content:	Supreme Court cases (1939–present) Court of Appeals cases (1939–present)
	Update:	As received from the court; usually daily
Westlaw www.westlaw.com *Commercial*	Content:	Supreme Court cases (1846–present) Court of Appeals cases (1907–present) Supreme Court briefs and petitions (1990– present)
	Update:	As received from the court; usually within a few days

Chapter 3

Digests and Finding Cases

After reading this chapter you will be able to:
- find cases in digests;
- use West topics and key numbers to expand or focus your case law research;
- understand the relationship between case headnotes and digests; and
- find cases online.

Researchers can locate Georgia cases in several ways: (1) through the West digests in print or online; (2) through secondary sources like legal periodicals, treatises, encyclopedias, and *American Law Reports* (A.L.R.) annotations, all of which refer to cases; (3) in annotations following the text of each statute in *Official Code of Georgia Annotated* and *West's Code of Georgia Annotated*; and (4) online by searching full-text case law databases. Secondary sources are explained in Chapter 8, and statutory research is explained in Chapter 4. This chapter discusses using West digests and finding cases online.

I. West Digests

Digests are indexes to case law. Digests contain abstracts or "digests" of cases organized by subject. Digests are particularly useful for identifying cases when you are researching a legal issue (such as joint custody) or concept (such as libel).

The digests discussed in this chapter are published by West. Although other companies also publish digests, West has the largest system—the only one that covers all American jurisdictions. You will often obtain the best results by using digests in conjunction with on-line systems, but let us examine how to use a digest alone to find the information you need.

The digest contains a comprehensive list of legal topics. Each legal topic is subdivided into issues, and each issue is assigned a digest classification number called a key number. Listed under each key number are headnotes from reported cases addressing the issue. Remember that West attorney-editors create headnotes by isolating and summarizing every issue of law that appears in the opinion and assigning topics and key numbers to each headnote. Each headnote is assigned at least one topic and key number, and some headnotes are assigned several.

Understanding the relationship between the headnotes and the digests is crucial to using the digests. The paragraphs in the digests are the headnote paragraphs from the cases in the reporters, rearranged according to subject. Headnotes from different cases that discuss the same point of law appear together in a digest, and the same headnote may appear in two or more places in the digest. Although the language is usually copied loosely from the text of the case, headnotes are written by West attorney-editors, not judges, and should never be cited.

A. Understanding the West Key Number System

West organizes its digests according to the West Key Number System. In this system, the entire body of law is broken down into general topics (for example, "Animals"). Each topic is further divided into points of law (for example, persons liable for injuries). A key number is assigned to each point of law. The key number 54 covers persons liable for injuries caused by animals. Therefore, under "Animals 54" in a digest, you will find cases that deal with persons liable for injuries caused by animals.

You must use both parts, the topic and the key number, in order to use the digests. The beauty of the West Key Number System is that the key number assigned to a point of law is uniform throughout all of West's digests. As a result, when you find a relevant case in the *Georgia Digest*, for example, you can look under the same topic and key number in any other West digest and find other relevant cases. Keep in mind, however, that a particular regional or state digest may not list any cases under a particular topic and key number because no cases have been classified under that topic and key number in that jurisdiction.

B. Choosing the Correct Digest

Your first step in using the digests is to choose the correct jurisdiction for your research. Refer to Table 3-1 for choosing a digest.

Table 3-1. Choosing a Digest

Jurisdiction	West Digests and Coverage
State	A digest is available for each state except Delaware, Nevada, and Utah. For Delaware, use the *Atlantic Digest*. For Nevada and Utah, use the *Pacific Digest*.
Regional	*Atlantic Digest* *North Eastern Digest* (discontinued by publisher) *North Western Digest* *Pacific Digest* *South Eastern Digest* *Southern Digest* (discontinued by publisher) For those states not covered in a regional digest, use the individual state digests.
Federal (lower federal courts and the U.S. Supreme Court)	*Federal Digest* (all cases prior to 1939) *Modern Federal Practice Digest* (1939–1961) *Federal Practice Digest 2d* (1961–1975) *Federal Practice Digest 3d* (1975–1988) *Federal Practice Digest 4th* (1989–present)
U.S. Supreme Court	*United States Supreme Court Digest* (1754–present)
American Digest System (all cases, both federal and state)	*Century Digests* (1658–1896) *First - Eleventh Decennial Digest* (1897–2004) *General Digests 11th* (2004–present)

The scope of most West digests is based on jurisdiction, although there are a few topical ones, for example, education law. The current digests for Georgia are the *Georgia Digest 2d* and the *South Eastern Digest 2d*.

Georgia Digest's first series (blue binding) covers 1792 to 1941, and the second series (green binding) covers 1942 to the present. A researcher should always begin with the most recent series and then continue to the earlier ones. Unless you are doing an exhaustive search, you may not need to use the first series. The *Georgia Digest* presents references to published cases decided by the Georgia Supreme Court, the Georgia Court of Appeals, and the U.S. District Courts in Georgia; cases arising from Georgia that result in opinions of the U.S. Court of Appeals for the Eleventh Circuit (formerly the Fifth Circuit before October 1, 1981); and Georgia cases that result in opinions of the U.S. Supreme Court.

The *South Eastern Digest* includes case digests from the following states: Georgia, North Carolina, South Carolina, Virginia, and West Virginia. The first series covers cases decided before 1935, and the second series covers cases from 1935 to the present. As with the *Georgia Digest*, begin with the second series. Unlike the *Georgia Digest*, the *South Eastern Digest* does not include citations to federal cases, just state cases.

The entries in both the *Georgia Digest* and the *South Eastern Digest* are the headnote paragraphs from the cases in the *South Eastern Reporter* rearranged according to subject. The paragraphs under each key number follow by jurisdiction, beginning with the federal courts, then the Georgia Supreme Court, and finally the Georgia Court of Appeals. Under each jurisdiction, the digests list the cases in reverse chronological order. This order is helpful because recent cases, which are listed first, are more likely to be pertinent to your research.

At the beginning of each headnote is a court abbreviation and date. The abbreviations are explained in tables at the beginning of each digest volume. Some of the court abbreviations used in the *Georgia Digest 2d* headnotes are noted in Table 3-2, in the order they would have appeared under one topic and key number.

Table 3-2. Court Abbreviations in *Georgia Digest 2d*

C.A.11 (Ga) 1990	1990 case decided by the Eleventh Circuit Court of Appeals
Ga. 1942	1942 case decided by the Supreme Court of Georgia
Ga.App. 1991	1991 case decided by the Court of Appeals of Georgia
Ga.App. 1989	1989 case decided by the Court of Appeals of Georgia

At the end of the digest headnote are citations to any statutes that are cited in the case. This information is followed by the case citation and any parallel citations. The excerpt in Table 3-3 is an example from the *Georgia Digest 2d*.

When researching Georgia law, you should first select the *Georgia Digest*, since it will provide you with the quickest way to determine case law in one state. The *South Eastern Digest* would be useful when you need cases from neighboring jurisdictions. A good practice is to use the most specific possible digest.

II. Using the Digests

How you use a digest depends on the information you already have from previous research. This section explains five methods: starting with "one good case;" using the Descriptive-Word Index; using the topic method; using the Table of Cases; and referring to the Words and Phrases volume.

A. Starting with One Good Case

Many times, you will have a great case that you found in a secondary source or one recommended by a colleague. If you are lucky enough to know one relevant case, you can easily expand your research by using the West Key Number System in the West digests. From your case, determine the relevant topics and key numbers and then look in the Georgia digest to find cases that have head-notes classified under those topics and key numbers. All West digests use the same topics and key numbers, so "one good case" can be from any jurisdiction. Notice the relationship between the head-note in a case in Table 3-4 and the digest paragraph pointed out in the digest in Table 3-3.

Table 3-3. Georgia Digest 2d

ANIMALS ⌐══ 55

see Descriptive-Word Index

maintenance of the stock, that permissible infer-ence disappears.
    John Hewell Trucking Co., Inc. v. Brock,
        522 S.E.2d 270, 239 Ga.App. 862.

    For the evidence to require a verdict for live-stock owner in negligence action, it must demand a finding that owner was not negligent in any re-spect; jury question reappears in the case where, although evidence of facts showing ordinary care on owner's part have been introduced, other facts would support a contrary inference.
    John Hewell Trucking Co., Inc. v. Brock,
        522 S.E.2d 270, 239 Ga.App. 862.

    Ga.App. 1974. Allegations and evidence that dog owner had allowed dog to run at large in neighborhood and had known that dog had chased other people was insufficient to show negligence on part of owner or that owner was liable for in-juries sustained when dog allegedly caused plain-tiff to be thrown to the ground.
Code, § 105-110
    Penick v. Grimsley, 204 S.E.2d 510, 130
        Ga.App. 722.

Reprinted from the *Georgia Digest 2d* with permission of Thomson/West.

Table 3-4. Relationship Between Headnote in Case and Digest Entry in Table 3-3

c

Penick v. Grimsley
130 Ga.App. 722, 204 S.E.2d 510
Ga.App. 1974.
January 30, 1974 (Approx. 1 page)

FOR EDUCATIONAL USE ONLY
West Reporter Image (PDF)

130 Ga.App. 722, 204 S.E.2d 510

Court of Appeals of Georgia, Division No. 1.

Aaron PENICK
v.
Sallie M. GRIMSLEY.
No. 48902.
Jan. 30, 1974.

Plaintiff brought action against dog owner for injuries allegedly sustained when dog caused her to be thrown to the ground. The State Court of Stephens County, Robert H. Harris, J., denied defendant's motion for summary judgment and the defendant appealed. The Court of Appeals, Quillian, J., held that allegations and evidence that defendant had allowed dog to run at large in neighborhood and that defendant knew that dog had chased other people were insufficient to show any negligence on part of defendant or liability for injuries sustained by plaintiff. Reversed.

West Headnotes

KeyCite Notes

28 Animals
28k47 Running at Large
28k55 k. Actions. Most Cited Cases

Allegations and evidence that dog owner had allowed dog to run at large in neighborhood and had known that dog had chased other people was insufficient to show negligence on part of owner or that owner was liable for injuries sustained when dog allegedly caused plaintiff to be thrown to the ground. Code, § 105-110.

Reprinted from Westlaw with permission of Thomson/West.

B. Using the Descriptive-Word Index

If you do not have one good case by which to find other cases, your gateway into the digest can be the Descriptive-Word Index (DWI). The DWI is a long list of everyday words, legal terms, and phrases. Under these DWI terms, you can find relevant topics and key numbers. This process is outlined in Table 3-5.

Before you use the DWI, analyze your fact situation thoroughly in order to generate sufficient research terms to look up in the DWI. You cannot use the DWI effectively if you do not fully understand your fact situation, because you may overlook important terms.

1. Develop Research Terms

Suppose that your client is the parent of a child who was injured by an unleashed pit bull in a Georgia city. The client wants you to file a claim against the owner of the dog and the local humane society, which was contractually responsible for enforcing the leash laws. You

---

Table 3-5. Outline for Digest Research
with the Descriptive-Word Index

---

1. Develop a list of research terms.

2. Find the research terms in the DWI, which will list topics and key numbers relevant to those terms.

3. Check the pocket part to the DWI.

4. Review each topic and key number in the main volumes of the digest.

5. Update each topic and key number by checking the pocket part or volume supplement, the cumulative supplementary pamphlets, and the digests contained in the reporters' most recent advance sheets.

6. Read all the relevant cases that your research reveals.

Table 3-6. Research Terms

Common Elements	Elements of this Problem	Research Terms
Parties	the owner of the pit bull, the child, and the humane society	dog owner injured child humane society
Places and things	the event took place in the city, a child was injured, and an unleashed dog was involved	city unleashed dog bite pit bulls
Potential claims and defenses	the owner of the pit bull was negligent in allowing the dog to run loose, and the humane society was negligent in failing to apprehend the loose dog the humane society claims that it had no knowledge of the dog running loose	negligence strict liability assumption of the risk contributory negligence "absence of care"
Relief	compensation for personal injuries	compensation for personal injuries

can develop a list of research terms by using the organized brain-storming approach introduced in Chapter 1. See Table 3-6 for a list of terms in the pit bull hypothetical.

2. Find the Terms in the DWI

Look for each research term in the DWI. For example, beginning with the DWI in the *Georgia Digest 2d*, you might look under the term "pit bulls." You will find that pit bulls are not listed. This term is too restrictive, so you must think of alternative terms. You should broaden your research term to "animals." When you look in the DWI under "ANIMALS," you will find the entry "Running at large." This entry will lead you to the topic "Animals" and key numbers 52–55, as shown in Table 3-7.

Table 3-7. Entry in Descriptive-Word Index in *Georgia Digest 2d*

ANIMALS

Running at large, Anim 52-55

-Injuries by animals at large

-Persons liable for injuries

Reprinted with permission of Thomson/West.

3. Check the Pocket Parts to the DWI

The information included in the Descriptive-Word Index will be only as current as the copyright date of that digest volume. To include new annotations and key numbers without reprinting an entire bound volume, the publisher prints *pocket parts*. These additional pages are inserted into a slot in the back cover of the bound volume. Pocket parts are printed annually. To be thorough, you must search these pocket parts for each of your research terms, and record any topics and key numbers you find. If the volume has been printed within the last year, however, it will not have a pocket part for you to check.

4. Review Each Topic and Key Number in the Main Volumes of the Digest

The next step is to pull the *Georgia Digest 2d* volume containing "Animals" off the shelf and turn to key numbers 52-55. Note that the spine of each digest volume does not list all the topics included in that volume. For example, in *Georgia Digest 2d*, the topic "Animals" appears in volume 1. The spine of that volume lists the topics "Alteration of Instruments" to "Appeal and Error," indicating that the volume includes those topics and others that come between them alphabetically.

At the beginning of each topic, you will find a list of Subjects Included as well as Subjects Excluded and Covered by Other Topics. These lists will help you decide whether that topic is likely to index

Table 3-8. Analysis Outline in the Digest

```
ANIMALS

Analysis

1.5  Animals as property; status.

 (1) In general

 (2) Wild animals in unconfined state, in general

 (3) Captured, confined or domesticated animals,
     in general

 (4) Dogs

 (5) Horses, cattle, sheep and other livestock

 (6) Birds and fowl
```

Reprinted with permission of Thomson/West.

cases most relevant to your research. The list of excluded subjects may contain references to other relevant topics found elsewhere in the digest.

If the topic has been expanded and renumbered to reflect current developments in the law, there will be a key number translation table reflecting the new key numbers.

Under the heading "Analysis," there is an outline of the topic as seen in Table 3-8. Longer topics will contain a short, summary outline and then a detailed outline. Many topics follow a general litigation organization, so that elements, defenses, pleadings, and evidence are discussed in that order.

You should take a moment to skim the Analysis outline to ensure that you found in the Descriptive-Word Index all the relevant key numbers within that topic. For example, in the hypothetical involving injury to a child by a pit bull, several key numbers are appropriate:

  54 - Personal liability for injuries
  55 - Actions
  56 - Penalties for violations of regulations
  57 - Criminal prosecutions

Once you are convinced that you have the correct key numbers, then turn to each of the relevant key numbers and review the case headnotes there. Write down the citation for each case that you decide you need to read. If parallel citations are given, write down both citations so that if the volume you need from one reporter is not on the shelves you can easily find the case using the parallel cite in the other reporter. At this point, the cites that you include in your notes do not have to be complete or conform to any system of citation. They simply need to provide enough information so that you are able to find the correct case. Recording the last name of one party, the volume, reporter, and page number will often be sufficient.

The process of reviewing headnotes and recording possibly relevant case citations can be tedious. However, your painstaking review of headnotes is essential. To analyze your client's situation accurately, you need to read every relevant case. Hurrying through the digest pages will allow you to end sooner, but the risk of missing crucial cases is too high.

However, you may be selective in deciding which cases to read first. Additionally, when a topic-key number contains many pages of case headnotes, or when you are working under tight deadlines, you may have to be selective in choosing the cases you are able to read. First, read those cases that are binding authority in your jurisdiction. Within that subset, read the most recent cases. Some headnotes include facts, and a case with facts similar to yours should be included in your written analysis of your client's situation. Never disregard a factually similar case simply because that case reaches a result that would be bad for your client. You must either find a way to distinguish that case or find an alternative legal basis for your claim.

5. Check Pocket Parts for Each Topic and Key Number

Again, the topics, key numbers, and case headnotes indexed in the digest are only as current as the volume's publication date. Recent information is most often provided through pocket parts. If the information is too thick to fit into a pocket part, the publisher will instead provide a soft-cover volume of recent material, which will be shelved next to the volume that it supplements.

Pocket parts are in turn kept current using *cumulative supplementary pamphlets*. These pamphlets contain information for all topics, so they generally are shelved after all of the volumes in the digest. These cumulative supplements are published periodically. The cover of a cumulative supplement will indicate both its publication date and the date of the pocket parts it supplements. You must check the supplement each time you do research using the digests in order to find the relevant cases that occasionally appear there. The outside cover of the pocket part or the supplementary pamphlet will indicate "Covering Cases Reported through volume [number] of the S.E.2d."

Finally, you may find coverage after these cumulative supplements by going to a particular reporter's most recent volumes and advance sheets, and using the digest contained in each. To do this, check inside the cover of the latest digest supplement to determine the last reporter volume included. You may rarely find your topic included in the advance sheet digests for the reporter, but you will find the most current information in print there.

In summary, to be sure that you have found all the cases using your topic and key number, you should check (1) the main digest volumes, (2) the pocket parts, (3) the cumulative supplementary pamphlet, and (4) the corresponding reporters and advance sheets not covered by the digest. Of course, there will always be some window of time between publication and release of the most current information. To insure currency, you must go to an online database, such as LexisNexis or Westlaw. You may also find cases that are more recent on Westlaw using the same topic and key number as you used in the books. Finding cases online is discussed in Part III of this chapter.

6. Read the Relevant Cases that Your Research Reveals

You must read the relevant cases that you found in your digest search. In fact, unless you have specific instructions to provide only a list of cases that may be relevant, your primary task will be to analyze the cases and apply them to your client's situation. Review Chapter 2 on analyzing individual cases.

Reading the cases and understanding the law will be easier if you organize your approach. First, review your list of all the cases that you found. You may notice some cases appear twice because they were indexed under several topics or key numbers. Strike out the duplicates so that you will not accidentally read the same case twice. Next, organize groups of cases according to jurisdiction and then by decision date. Learning how the law developed over time in each jurisdiction will be easier if you read the cases chronologically. On the other hand, finding the current rule of law will likely be easier if you begin with the most recent cases. Define your goal and organize the order in which you read the cases accordingly.

Then go to the reporters and find each case you have listed, or locate the text of the cases in an online database. Quickly skim the synopsis to see whether the case appears to be on point. Find each relevant headnote and turn to that part of the case. Skim that portion of the case. Only when you have skimmed the relevant parts of a case should you consider photocopying, printing, or taking notes from it. Do not waste paper, money, or your time by delaying the difficult work of analyzing cases.

In addition to taking notes on individual cases, pay attention to how the cases fit together. Look for trends in the law and in the facts of the cases. Has the law remained unchanged or have new elements been introduced? Has the meaning of an important term been redefined? Have certain facts virtually guaranteed success for one party while other facts have tended to cause difficulties? Does one case summarize the current rule, or do you have to synthesize a rule from several cases that each address part of the rule?

C. Using the Topic Method

If you analyze your client's legal problem in terms of a subject area, such as animals, you can go directly to the volume of the digest that includes the topic "Animals." Next you would read the Analysis that appears at the beginning of the text of each topic (see Table 3-8) until you find the appropriate entry.

The topic approach is most appropriate for experienced researchers who are familiar with the legal topics that are presented in a problem. Novice researchers may not select the best topics and key numbers because of lack of familiarity with all of the subject area possibilities.

D. Using the Table of Cases

If you know only the name of the case you want to read, the Table of Cases is easy to use and will lead you to the correct reporter and page number. Every digest has its own Table of Cases. When you also know the jurisdiction of the case you want to read, use the Table of Cases volumes at the end of the digest for that jurisdiction.

In addition to providing you with the correct citation information for the case, the Table of Cases also lists topics and key numbers under which that case has been classified.

If the case you are looking for was decided during the previous year, you may find the citation in the pocket parts to the Table of Cases in the digests, or you may have to check the Table of Cases Reported in the advance sheets to the reporter in which you expect the case to be published.

E. Words and Phrases

To learn whether a court has *defined* a term, refer to the Words and Phrases volumes at the end of the digest. West also publishes a multi-volume set, *Words and Phrases*, containing court definitions from all federal and state jurisdictions combined. While a dictionary like *Black's Law Dictionary* will provide a general definition of a term, *Words and Phrases* will direct you to a case that defines the term for a particular jurisdiction. Judicial definitions are especially helpful when an important term in a statute is vague. At the end of each entry in the Words and Phrases volumes, West lists the topics and key numbers used for that case's headnotes.

III. Finding Cases Online

LexisNexis and Westlaw are the largest commercial providers of computerized legal research. Both companies have good training programs for law students on how to locate cases. They also provide some free online training for all subscribers.

The other commercial providers for Georgia case law are Casemaker and Loislaw. Casemaker is an online research tool by Lawriter and the Ohio Bar Association. Casemaker is free to Georgia bar members. Loislaw is a low-cost alternative to find case law and other materials. Although there are government websites, the Georgia Supreme Court and Court of Appeals websites have limited search capabilities due to very limited coverage. The Georgia Supreme Court website includes cases from the last few years, and the Georgia Court of Appeals website includes cases from the most recent five years.

LexisNexis, Westlaw, Casemaker, and Loislaw offer two search methods: Natural Language, and Terms and Connectors. In all four systems, you will get better results with Terms and Connectors. The search method that is best for your needs is determined by several factors, including the type of information you are looking for. The guidelines in Table 3-9 can help you determine which search method to use.

A. Natural Language

The Natural Language search method allows you to use plain English to retrieve relevant documents. Enter a description of your issue and the online systems will display the documents that best match the concepts in your description. The online systems identify legal phrases in your description (such as "quantum meruit," "adverse possession," and "state of mind"), remove common terms (such as "is" and "for"), and generate variations of terms (such as "defamed," "defaming," and "defamation" for "defame").

Table 3-9. Determining Whether to Use Natural Language,
or Terms and Connectors Searching

Use Natural Language when you are ...	Use Terms and Connectors when you are ...
... searching for broad concepts.	... searching for particular terms.
... searching databases containing large numbers of documents, and you want to retrieve a small number of documents to review.	... searching for a particular document.
... a new or infrequent online user or unfamiliar with Boolean logic (Terms and Connectors).	... searching for all documents containing specific information, such as all opinions written by a particular Georgia judge.
... not retrieving the information you are looking for by using a Terms and Connectors search.	

B. Terms and Connectors

When you search the online systems using the Terms and Connectors search method, you enter a query consisting of key terms from your issue and connectors specifying the relationship between those terms. These connectors are explained in Chapter 10.

IV. Searching Westlaw Using Custom Digest and KeySearch

Westlaw's Custom Digest contains the complete topic and key number outline used by West attorney-editors to classify headnotes. The Custom Digest helps you identify topics and key numbers related to your issue and retrieve cases with headnotes classified under those topics and key numbers. All headnotes classified under a specific topic and key number are contained in a single document. To use the Custom Digest, first click on "Site Map," then "Key Number Digest," and follow the directions.

KeySearch is a another research tool that helps you find cases and secondary sources within a specific area of the law. KeySearch guides you through the selection of terms from a classification system based on the West Key Number System and then uses the key numbers and their underlying concepts to run a query, which was created by a West attorney-editor for you to use. To use Westlaw's Key-Search, first click on "Site Map," then "KeySearch," and follow the directions.

V. Searching LexisNexis Using Search Advisor and Easy Search

A unique way to search for cases on LexisNexis is with Search Advisor. Search Advisor is a legal information-finding tool that is based on a classification system that organizes more than 16,000 legal topics by area of law. It can help you target your legal issue, identify an appropriate research source, and formulate your search request. For example, if you are looking for cases on peer review in a healthcare setting, but you are unsure where to search, you can type "peer review" in Look for a Legal Topic. Search Advisor will lead you to the topic "Healthcare Law" and subtopic "Business Administration and Organization." These topics can help you formulate your search request.

Additionally, if you are unsure of whether Terms and Connectors or Natural Language is the best search strategy for your query, you can select the Easy Search radio button and let LexisNexis identify the best search engine based on the terms you have entered. Easy Search is optimized for two to three search terms and will recognize phrases in quotes as well as legal citations.

VI. Searching Casemaker

You can search on Casemaker using the basic search or the advanced search. With the advanced search, you will use a template and easily fill in different fields. Casemaker uses Terms and Connectors, but, instead of using "and/or/but," it has its own symbols, as shown in Table 3-10. You will typically achieve better results if you use connectors and the advanced search on Casemaker.

Table 3-10. Casemaker Connectors

Function	Casemaker Connector
and	space
phrase	" "
or	,
but	-

Chapter 4

Statutes, Constitutions, and Court Rules

After reading this chapter, you will be able to:

- find a Georgia statute in one of the two print codes;
- locate a Georgia session law in print sources;
- locate Georgia codes and session laws online;
- find federal statutes;
- locate Georgia and federal constitutions; and
- find Georgia and federal court rules.

I. Codes

Statutory laws are classified — that is, codified — by subject or topic in volumes called codes. These codes group the laws by subject and show all subsequent amendments. You will use an annotated code (discussed in Part II) when you want to locate statutes with all of their amendments and deletions, along with notes of decisions applying the statute.

To locate laws efficiently, you need a basic understanding of how the codes are organized. Laws are collected and organized by subject matter into titles. Each title of the code is further divided into subdivisions called chapters and sections. For example, Georgia laws pertaining to arson are classified under title 16. The law that specifically addresses first degree arson is in chapter 7, section 60 of that title. Thus, the citation would read O.C.G.A. § 16-7-60.

Since some laws apply to more than one subject, you may have to check more than one place in the code. In addition to placing similar laws together under topics, codes also incorporate amendments and indicate repealed laws by stating that the law was repealed by a different code section.

II. Georgia Statutes

Georgia has two annotated codes: the *Official Code of Georgia Annotated* (O.C.G.A.), published by LexisNexis, and *West's Code of Georgia Annotated* (Ga. Code Ann.), published by West. Both contain the text of Georgia's statutes, citations to cases that discuss the statutes, and other research references. The *Official Code of Georgia Annotated* is the code legislatively sanctioned by O.C.G.A. § 1-1-1 (2002) as official. However, you should check both sources, if accessible, since each source might have different annotations and citations to secondary materials. Appendix 4-A at the end of this chapter compares the features of these two codes.

Until the early 1980s, the Harrison Company published the only code, *Georgia Code Annotated* (commonly referred to as the Code of 1933, when it was first published). However, in 1976 the Code Revision Study Committee recommended a complete revision of the code. The legislature contracted with the Michie Company, which LexisNexis later acquired, to work with the state in preparing a new official code. During a special session in 1981, the Georgia General Assembly adopted the results of this effort, the *Official Code of Georgia Annotated*. This code became effective on November 1, 1982.

A. *Official Code of Georgia Annotated*

As noted earlier, the *Official Code of Georgia Annotated* (O.C.G.A.), often called the Code of 1981, is divided into major subject areas called titles. The titles are subdivided into chapters that, in turn, are divided further into sections. Each section contains the actual language of the law. According to O.C.G.A. § 1-1-8(e), the proper citation format reads, for example, "O.C.G.A. § 20-2-16 (year)."[1]

O.C.G.A. includes only laws of general applicability. Local and special acts are not codified and appear only in the session laws, *Georgia Laws*. A local act is a measure that applies to a specific city, county, or special district named in the act. Special acts are not currently used. However, volume 42 of O.C.G.A. indexes any existing special acts and current local laws.

The Tables volume in O.C.G.A. allows you to convert a citation from the now-defunct Harrison's *Georgia Code Annotated* to O.C.G.A. A citation to the old code is recognized easily by two numbers separated by a hyphen, e.g., Ga. Code Ann. § 43-3323 (1976). Volume 41 includes conversion charts from Ga. Code Ann. (labeled 1933 Code) to O.C.G.A. (labeled 1981 Code) and the reverse. You cannot covert an old code citation to an O.C.G.A. citation online, so you have to use volume 41.

Each volume of O.C.G.A. has an annual pocket part for updating statutory provisions. Pocket parts fit into pockets in the back cover of each volume. The pocket parts are arranged by the same section numbers as the bound volume.

However, since the publishers issue the pocket parts during the summer and the legislative session extends from January to March, there will be a few months when a new law or amendment is not yet included in the print O.C.G.A. To fill this gap between the annual pocket part and the recently enacted laws, use one of these publications: the red softbound *Georgia Laws*, the *Advance Legislative Service* (LexisNexis), the *Georgia Legislative Service* (West), or the online services that include session laws. In addition, the Georgia General Assembly website at www.legis.state.ga.us includes bills signed by the Governor; however, you must know the bill number to locate the law or search by keyword, which can be cumbersome.

---

1. The citation format required by the courts as stated in O.C.G.A. differs from the citation format required in *The Bluebook: A Uniform System of Citation* 206 Table T.1. The *Bluebook* policy is not to adopt local citation rules for state codes.

To find more recent references to cases that interpret the statutes, you should use the *Advance Annotation Service* (LexisNexis) or the *Interim Annotation Service* (West). These cumulative pamphlets supplement the annual pocket parts of the codes with new notes to judicial decisions and other research references. This service does not carry the text of the new laws, only the new annotations. You should consult the online services for the most recent interpretive decisions for statutes.

B. *West's Code of Georgia Annotated*

In 2003, West published a new code, *West's Code of Georgia Annotated*. An example of a proper citation to this code is "Ga. Code Ann. § 16-7-60 (West 2003)." Appendix 4-A to this chapter compares the features of this code to the official code. *West's Code of Georgia Annotated* includes the same numbering system as O.C.G.A. West's attorney-editors thoroughly examined the text of the statutes and prepared thousands of annotations to cases and secondary materials, along with extensive index references to ensure thorough access to the code. Since the West publishers realize that an index to a code can be troublesome, West uses many cross-references to common terms. For example, the common term "Lemon Law" in the index refers you to "Ga. Code Ann. § 10-1-780." You should always cite to O.C.G.A., even if you are using Ga. Code Ann.

C. The Research Process Using Print Codes

How you begin to research Georgia statutes depends on the information you have as you begin your work. Sometimes, especially early in your career, an attorney may tell you exactly which statute controls your client's situation. Your supervising attorney may know from experience that O.C.G.A. § 16-7-60 deals with arson. In that case, review the spines of the *Official Code of Georgia Annotated* volumes to find the one that contains the chapter for that statute; then look through that volume numerically to find the statute. Statute numbers are included on the top, outside corner of each page. Using *West's*

Table 4-1. Researching the Georgia Code in Print

1. Develop a list of research terms.
2. Search the index.
3. Find and read the statutory language.
4. Update the section of the code.
5. Find cases that interpret or apply statutes.

Code of Georgia Annotated works the same way. If you do not know the citation of the relevant statutes, follow the steps in Table 4-1.

1. Develop a List of Research Terms

To find all the statutes that may relate to your issue, develop a list of research terms, as explained in Chapter 1. Consider the parties, places and things, potential claims, and relief. For example, if a person were charged with attempting to burn a house, you would list the following terms: arsonist, house, fire, arson, burn.

2. Search the Index

Take these research terms to the index volumes shelved at the end of the code. As you find the terms in the index volumes, write down any statutory references given.

Do not stop reviewing the index after finding just one statutory reference; several statutes may address your issue. Sometimes a research term will be included in the index but will be followed by a cross-reference to another index term. For example, the term "fire" refers you to "arson." Referring to that term may lead you to relevant statutes. Table 4-2 includes index sections covering arson.

Table 4-2. Arson in the O.C.G.A. Index

ARSON, §§ 16-7-60 to 16-7-62

3. Find and Read the Statutory Language

Review the spines of O.C.G.A. or Ga. Code Ann. to find the volume that contains the title and chapter number of the statute. Remember that the chapters are the second number given in statutory citations. Then look up the section number to find your statute.

This next step is the most important: *Read* the statute very carefully. Too many researchers fail to take the time necessary to read the language of the statute and consider all its implications before deciding whether it is relevant to the research problem. Moreover, because few statutes are so clear that they can be understood with one reading, careful research may require you to read a statute several times before you understand its meaning and relevance.

To understand a single statute you may have to read other, related statutes. One statute may contain general provisions while another contains definitions. Yet another statute may contain exceptions to the general rule.

To guarantee that you understand the statute, break it into elements. Using bullet points or an outline format is helpful for identifying key ideas. Connecting words and punctuation provide guidance for the relationships between the different requirements of the statute. Small words like "and" and "or" can drastically change the meaning of the statute. With "and," all statutory requirements must be present for the statute to apply; with "or," only one part is needed. Note, too, the difference between "shall," which requires action, and "may," which is permissive. Table 4-3 includes a passage from O.C.G.A. that is broken into various elements, and Table 4-4 includes excerpts from the code on LexisNexis.

4. Update the Section of the Code

The constant possibility of change in legislation means that you must always check a law for recent changes. Look at the publication date (the copyright date on the back of the title page) of the hardbound volume of the code to determine whether a law needs updating.

Table 4-3. Elements of First Degree Arson

- a person
- by means of fire or explosive
- knowingly
  - damages or
  - causes, aids, abets, advises, encourages, hires, counsels, or procures another to damage
- dwelling house, building, vehicle, railroad car, watercraft, aircraft, or other structure

To check for amendments and deletions that have appeared since the bound volume was published, refer to the pocket parts inserted in the back of each volume. The pocket parts are arranged by the same section numbers as the bound volume. Also, check any supplementary pamphlets shelved at the end of the set.

5. Find Cases that Interpret or Apply Statutes

It is rare to locate a relevant statute and apply it immediately to your client's facts without having first to research case law. Legislatures write broad statutes to apply to a wide array of circumstances. To be able to predict how a court may apply a statute to your client's specific facts, you must know how the courts have interpreted the statute and applied it in the past.

Listed under Notes of Decisions are short summaries of cases that have interpreted and applied that statute. Usually, the summaries are organized by subject areas. Each summary concludes with the name of the case, followed by a citation. The citation indicates which court decided the case and where it can be found. You must record the citation information accurately to enable you to find the cases in the reporters. To find the most recent annotations, remember to check pocket parts and supplementary pamphlets.

Table 4-4. Excerpt from the Georgia Code on LexisNexis

O.C.G.A. § 16-7-60 (2007)

§ 16-7-60. Arson in the first degree

(a) A person commits the offense of arson in the first degree when, by means of fire or explosive, he or she knowingly damages or knowingly causes, aids, abets, advises, encourages, hires, counsels, or procures another to damage:

(1) Any dwelling house of another without his or her consent or in which another has a security interest, including but not limited to a mortgage, a lien, or a conveyance to secure debt, without the consent of both, whether it is occupied, unoccupied, or vacant;

(2) Any building, vehicle, railroad car, watercraft, or other structure of another without his or her consent or in which another has a security interest, including but not limited to a mortgage, a lien, or a conveyance to secure debt, without the consent of both, if such structure is designed for use as a dwelling, whether it is occupied, unoccupied, or vacant;

(3) Any dwelling house, building, vehicle, railroad car, watercraft, aircraft, or other structure whether it is occupied, unoccupied, or vacant and when such is insured against loss or damage by fire or explosive and such loss or damage is accomplished without the consent of both the insurer and the insured;

(4) Any dwelling house, building, vehicle, railroad car, watercraft, aircraft, or other structure whether it is occupied, unoccupied, or vacant with the intent to defeat, prejudice, or defraud the rights of a spouse or co-owner; or

(5) Any building, vehicle, railroad car, watercraft, aircraft, or other structure under such circumstances that it is reasonably foreseeable that human life might be endangered.

(b) A person also commits the offense of arson in the first degree when, in the commission of a felony, by means of fire or explosive, he or she knowingly damages or knowingly causes, aids, abets, advises, encourages, hires, counsels, or procures another to damage anything included or described in subsection (a) of this Code section.

(c) A person convicted of the offense of arson in the first degree shall be punished by a fine of not more than $50,000.00 or by imprisonment for not less than one nor more than 20 years, or both.

HISTORY: Ga. L. 1924, p. 192, § 1; Code 1933, § 26-2208; Ga. L. 1949, p. 1118, § 2; Code 1933, § 26-1401, enacted by Ga. L. 1968, p. 1249, § 1; Ga. L. 1976, p. 1497, § 1; Ga. L. 1979, p. 935, § 1; Ga. L. 2004, p. 734, § 1/SB 184.

D. Session Laws — *Georgia Laws*

Occasionally, research requires the original statutory language as passed by the Georgia General Assembly. In addition, research may involve a repealed law that has been deleted from the code. Both of these research problems require reference to *session laws*, which are the laws as enacted by the Georgia legislature. Session laws are compiled and published under the title *Georgia Laws*. Initially, the new laws are published in red, softbound advance sheets. At the end of the legislative session, they are compiled in bound volumes.

Georgia Laws (1787–present) includes the Senate or House bill number and the text of the statute. The laws are printed in chronological order by date of enactment. The Georgia legislative procedure is covered in Chapter 5, which will aid in the understanding of the Georgia legislative process. Unless otherwise noted, laws in Georgia are effective July 1 of each year.

As enacted, an act contains a preamble or caption to the act that serves as a *purpose* clause that can be useful in determining the legislature's intent. Compilers of the *Georgia Laws* write the preamble or caption to let the reader know the subject of an act. However, these captions do not constitute part of the act; they are editorial enhancements added by the compilers.

Eventually, the annual bound volumes consolidate the materials in the red, softbound advance sheets. The first volume of *Georgia Laws* contains general laws, resolutions, and proposed amendments to the Georgia Constitution for a particular year. The second volume includes local laws, special laws, and resolutions for the same year. There may be a third volume for an extra legislative session. In addition to a topical index, a very useful table in *Georgia Laws* allows a researcher to learn whether legislators have amended, reversed, renumbered, or repealed a statutory section during that session. When interested in the summaries of legislative activity, you should use the pamphlet titled "Summary of General Statutes Enacted at the (year) Session of the General Assembly of Georgia." Table 4-5 is an excerpt from a 2004 act.

Table 4-5. Act on Georgia General Assembly Website

04 SB184/AP

Senate Bill 184
By: Senators Mullis of the 53rd, Hamrick of the 30th, Bowen of the 13th, Smith of the 52nd, Shafter of the 48th and others
AS PASSED

AN ACT

To amend Article 3 of Chapter 7 of Title 16 of the Official Code of Georgia Annotated, relating to arson and explosives, so as to provide for additional offenses constituting the crimes of arson in the first, second, and third degree; to provide an effective date; to provide for applicability; to repeal conflicting laws; and for other purposes.

BE IT ENACTED BY THE GENERAL ASSEMBLY OF GEORGIA:

SECTION 1.

Article 3 of Chapter 7 of Title 16 of the Official Code of Georgia Annotated, relating to arson and explosives, is amended by striking Code Section 16-7-60, relating to arson in the first degree, and inserting in its place a new Code Section 16-7-60 to read as follows:

"16-7-60.
(a) A person commits the offense of arson in the first degree when, by means of fire or explosive, he or she knowingly damages or knowingly causes, aids, abets, advises, encourages, hires, counsels, or procures another to damage:
(1) Any dwelling house of another without his or her consent or in which another has a security interest, including but not limited to a mortgage, a lien, or a conveyance to secure debt, without the consent of both, whether it is occupied, unoccupied, or vacant;
(2) Any building, vehicle, railroad car, watercraft, or other structure of another without his or her consent or in which another has a security interest, including but not limited to a mortgage, a lien, or a conveyance to secure debt, without the consent of both, if such structure is designed for use as a dwelling, whether it is occupied, unoccupied, or vacant;

Table 4-6. Online Sources of the Georgia Code and Sessions Laws

Source Name	Code or Session Laws	Web Address	Free or Commercial
Casemaker	Both	www.gabar.org	Free to members of the State Bar of Georgia
GALILEO Georgia Legislative Documents (1774–1995)	Session Laws	www.galileo.usg.edu	Available at Georgia educational institutions and public libraries
Georgia General Assembly, provided by LexisNexis	Both	www.legis.state.ga.us and click on "Georgia Code"	Free
LexisNexis	Both	www.lexis.com	Commercial
Loislaw	Both	www.loislaw.com	Commercial
Westlaw	Both	www.westlaw.com	Commercial

E. Using the Online Codes and Session Laws

The code and session laws are available online in various sources. Table 4-6 lists where you can find the code and session laws online. An expanded table appears in Appendices 4-B and 4-C to this chapter.

1. Using the Online Codes on LexisNexis and Westlaw

You may search both codes online by using search terms, code citation, the index, or the table of contents. O.C.G.A. is available on LexisNexis as a commercial source. LexisNexis also provides access to O.C.G.A. on the free Georgia General Assembly site. Ga. Code Ann. is a commercial source available on Westlaw.

You can use search terms by using Terms and Connectors or Natural Language. However, when searching for statutes online, you have to anticipate the language used by the legislature in writing the law. Searching the table of contents is often more productive than searching the entire database with your search terms.

On LexisNexis and Westlaw, the Georgia Statutory Table of Contents file provides the best option for online statutory research. The file allows you to retrieve code sections by navigating through the titles of the code. The table of contents also allows you to scroll through related sections of the code. Because statutory sections are part of a large code section, there can be many related sections.

When you access the Table of Contents file, the first level of the outline automatically appears. Each document contains a hierarchical outline with descriptive headings for the code sections. You can also use the file to find terms specific to the Georgia statutes and then use those terms to develop a full-text search. To browse the table of contents, click the plus (+) and the minus (-) symbols. To retrieve a specific section, click its hypertext link.

The Table of Contents file is particularly useful when you are searching for a very common legal term, for example, Contracts—statute of frauds. If you search the entire code using Natural Language, your search will retrieve too many hits. If you search only the Table of Contents file, you will easily locate O.C.G.A. § 13-5-30.

As an added enhancement on LexisNexis, information (enclosed in asterisks) regarding the date of a section indicates the most recent update to the statutes. On Westlaw, the current date is indicated at the end of the code section.

You may need to update a statute if the legislature is in session, or if the session laws have not yet been incorporated into the code. Once you are in the code database, you can KeyCite the law on Westlaw or Shepardize it on LexisNexis. The code is updated continuously during the legislative session.

2. *Other Online Sources*

The unannotated code (no cases or annotations) is available for free on the Georgia General Assembly website (provided by LexisNexis). On the General Assembly website, you can also search session laws by keyword, or, if you have a citation to the Senate or House bill number, you can search that way. Unfortunately, you cannot locate laws by public law number. To locate new laws amending a code section, search the section numbers, including the hyphens, for example 47-1-20. This website provides free access for all citizens to Georgia laws. The coverage of the laws begins in 1995 and updates are made continuously during the legislative session.

You can search for older Georgia session laws on GALILEO and on the Georgia General Assembly website. GALILEO stands for **GeorgiA LIbrary LEarning Online**, an initiative of the Board of Regents of the University System of Georgia. A web-based virtual library, GALILEO provides access to multiple information resources. On GALILEO, coverage of Georgia session laws goes back to 1774 and continues to 1999. This is the only online source for full retrospective coverage. Select the "Georgia" tab, click on "Laws & Legislation," and then select "Georgia Legislative Documents."

F. *Uniform Laws Annotated*

Georgia has adopted several uniform laws promulgated by the National Conference of Commissioners on Uniform State Laws. Interpretations from other state courts that have adopted the uniform law may be valuable as persuasive authority. The *Uniform Laws Annotated* (U.L.A.), published by West, contains this information.

The U.L.A. includes the text of each uniform law approved by the Commissioners, with each section of the act followed by the Commissioners' comments, citations to secondary sources, and digests of decisions. A table immediately precedes the text of each uniform act, showing the states that have adopted the act and the citation to the state law. You can identify the uniform laws by looking under the heading "Uniform Laws" in the indexes of O.C.G.A. and Ga. Code Ann. An alternative is to look in the Directory of Acts and Tables of Adopting Jurisdictions, a pamphlet published with the U.L.A.

G. Ordinances

Numerous Georgia cities and 159 Georgia counties exercise legislative functions. The state grants counties and municipalities some measure of control by home rule. Under the Georgia Constitution, Georgia grants to its cities and counties a great degree of self-governing power.

Table 4-7. Georgia Ordinances Online

Content	Web Address
Municipal Code Corporation (publishes ordinances for many Georgia cities and counties)	www.municode.com
List of contact information for counties and cities	www.georgia.gov (click on "Government" and then "Local Government")

In Georgia, two types of city and county laws exist: resolutions and ordinances. The courts have defined a resolution as dealing with matters of special or temporary character, for example, designating a day to honor a dignitary. An ordinance is legislation that deals with an ongoing situation in the city or county and sets a permanent rule or law, for example, the licensing of the sale of alcoholic beverages. Most of the highly populated cities and counties have published codifications or compilations of their ordinances. When these resources are not codified, a researcher can obtain county and city ordinances directly from the clerk's office. Table 4-7 lists the sources of online ordinances.

III. Researching the Statutes of Other States

The same basic process applies to statutory research in other states. Every state has an annotated code that you can use like O.C.G.A. In many states, however, the legislature meets biennially rather than annually. The result is that statutes are added, deleted, and modified every other year.

IV. Georgia Constitutions

Georgia's current constitution was adopted in November 1982 and became effective July 1983. It is the latest of eleven constitutions, with the first one written in 1777.

A. Researching in Print

The current 1983 Georgia Constitution is available in volume 2 of the *Official Code of Georgia Annotated* (O.C.G.A.) or volumes 2 and 3 of *West's Code of Georgia Annotated* (Ga. Code Ann.). As with federal constitutional research, judicial interpretation of the Georgia Constitution is voluminous. The O.C.G.A. and Ga. Code Ann. make available citations to court decisions interpreting the Georgia constitutions. A researcher may also find Georgia and federal cases and other sources citing the Georgia Constitution by using Shepard's and KeyCite.

In addition to providing annotations to judicial decisions, O.C.G.A. and Ga. Code Ann. include citations to opinions of the Attorney General, citations to law review articles, and citations to comparable 1976 constitutional provisions. These code volumes also include historical notes referring to the presence or absence of similar provisions in earlier documents that may be useful for research purposes. Volume 41 of O.C.G.A. provides tables comparing each provision of the earlier constitutions (1877, 1945, and 1976) to the 1983 constitution.

Article X of the Georgia Constitution stipulates amendment procedures. In addition, *Georgia Laws* includes resolutions of the General Assembly that propose amendments to the Georgia constitution. Once the legislature and Governor approve the amendments, the constitution incorporates the text of the amendments.

B. Researching Online

The Georgia Constitution is available online through a number of sources. Westlaw and LexisNexis provide annotated versions of the current constitution; their sites are updated frequently. Loislaw and Casemaker offer the text of the constitution, but no annotations. The Georgia Secretary of State's website has a .pdf version of the constitution without annotations. The Georgia code website is also an option for the unannotated constitution. Appendix 4-D of this chapter provides web addresses and summarizes the coverage of each online provider.

C. Citing the Georgia Constitution

The correct citation format for the current Georgia Constitution is, for example, "Ga. Const. art. I, § 9, para. 20 (2006)." Although citing the Georgia Constitution by referencing a code section would be more convenient, it is necessary to cite by article, section, and paragraph because the legislature has never codified the Georgia Constitution of 1983.

V. Georgia Court Rules

Georgia court rules, like other state court rules, are a set of procedural regulations adopted by the Georgia courts that are mandatory on the parties and their lawyers. The courts' rulemaking authority derives from their constitutional powers and legislative authority. The Supreme Court of Georgia has specific authority to establish, amend, and alter its own rules of practice. Likewise, the Georgia Constitution requires that the Court of Appeals and the lower courts have uniform rules of practice and procedure.

West prints an annual two-volume softbound set titled *Georgia Court Rules and Procedure—State and Federal.* Each volume is called a *deskbook* because its size makes it an easy reference tool. Its comprehensive index makes this publication very useful.

Another convenient location for court rules and case notes is the *Georgia Rules of Court Annotated,* published annually by LexisNexis. A similar source, titled *Georgia Court Manual Rules and Regulations Annotated* and published by Darby Printing Company in loose-leaf format, includes court rules, state bar rules, the code of judicial conduct, and rules of the Judicial Qualifications Commission. *West's Code of Georgia Annotated* also publishes court rules; however, the rules are not included in O.C.G.A.

Since changes in court rules are the result of court proceedings, advance sheets of the *Georgia Reports,* the *South Eastern Reporter,* and the *Georgia Cases* contain recent changes in court rules. Although there are many sources for updating legal materials, updating court rules is only available using Shepard's in print or online. Refer to Chapter 7 for an in-depth discussion of updating.

VI. Federal Research

A. Federal Codes

Similar to the Georgia codes, the federal codes are organized by title, chapter, and section.

1. Print Sources of the Federal Codes

The federal code is found in these publications:

- *United States Code* (U.S.C.), the official code for federal laws;
- *United States Code Service* (U.S.C.S.), published by Lexis-Nexis; and
- *United States Code Annotated* (U.S.C.A.), published by West.

For statutory research, you will probably want to use an annotated code, which contains the same text and numbering as the official U.S.C., and also provides notes of cases that have construed the statutes and references to regulations and secondary sources. An annotated code includes cross-references to related sections within the code and refers you to the research tools provided by its publisher.

2. United States Code

The U.S.C. is published by the U.S. Government Printing Office. The set is recompiled every six years, using the same fifty subject categories or titles. Congress has deemed the U.S.C. to be prima facie evidence of the law. While the U.S.C. has the advantage of being official, the unofficial *United States Code Annotated* (U.S.C.A.) and *United States Code Service* (U.S.C.S.) are more helpful research tools because the U.S.C. does not give citations to cases that have interpreted the statutes. Moreover, the U.S.C. will not be as current as you need. It is reissued every six years, with cumulative annual supplements between the new editions. In reality, the annual cumulative supplements do not appear in the library until eight months to two years have passed. Therefore, if you rely only on the U.S.C., you will miss current laws, amendments, and deletions.

Note that both the *Bluebook* and the *ALWD Citation Manual* recommend citing the official code when possible. See Appendix A at the end of this book for additional information on legal citation format.

3. U.S.C.A. and U.S.C.S.

The two annotated codes, U.S.C.A. and U.S.C.S., are quite similar. A small library may have just one of these series, and using either one is appropriate.

U.S.C.A. is an example of the West publishing philosophy. West believes in providing as much information as possible and giving researchers tools that help them use that information efficiently and effectively. U.S.C.A. fills more than 300 volumes and provides researchers with citations to cases and a wide variety of other references. Because each statute is followed by editorially enhanced notes and references to other research materials, U.S.C.A. is easy to use to find case references. U.S.C.A. is available online on Westlaw.

U.S.C.S., published by LexisNexis, also includes annotations to cases and other useful materials. U.S.C.S. fills 235 volumes and has numerous cross-references to the *Code of Federal Regulations*, treatises, and law review articles. U.S.C.S. has better coverage of citations to administrative decisions than U.S.C.A. Online access to U.S.C.S. is available on LexisNexis.

4. Finding Statutes in U.S.C.A. and U.S.C.S.

The following tips will help you use U.S.C.A. and U.S.C.S. in print. When you need a specific statute but know only the subject of the law, you will need to use the multi-volume General Index. It is important to consider alternative terms when using the index. The index includes many cross-references that can lead you to the correct statutory title and section.

If you know the popular name of an act or its acronym, you can check the Popular Name Table located at the end of the General Index. The popular name of an act is the name by which it is commonly known. Sometimes an act is commonly known by the name of its author. For example, the Sarbanes-Oxley Act of 2002 is named after its authors in Congress.

B. Session Laws

At the end of each session of Congress, the laws for that session are compiled and published in numerical order in bound volumes. As in Georgia, these laws are referred to as session laws. Session laws include preambles and other information that may be evidence of legislative intent, but these preambles are not codified.

Session laws are useful when you are looking for the original version of an act as it existed prior to its codification by subject in U.S.C. or before amendment, or when you require the language of a particular amendment.

You will also use session laws when you need to find laws that have been repealed and deleted from the current code. For example, assume that your client has been charged with committing a federal crime based on conduct that occurred several years ago. Assume further that the law applying to that conduct has changed since the conduct occurred. You will have to look for the law that applied at the time of the conduct.

You can locate federal session laws in these print sources:

- *United States Statutes at Large* (Stat.), the official session laws publication produced by the U.S. Government Printing Office. It is found in every law library, but—as is frequently true of government publications—it is slow to arrive, lagging several years behind the end of the session covered.
- Advance pamphlets to U.S.C.S. and advance pamphlets to U.S.C.A.
- *U.S. Code Congressional and Administrative News* (USCCAN), published by West. In addition to reprinting *Statutes at Large*, USCCAN includes selected legislative history material. It lists

citations for House, Senate, and conference committee reports and reprints the report or reports that West attorney-editors determine to be the most closely related to the law. USCCAN is available on Westlaw in the U.S. Code Congressional & Administrative News database.

A word of caution: You cannot safely use a session-law version of an act to determine present law after that act has been codified, since the original (session) law may have been subsequently repealed or amended. You will find the present text of a law in a code, as explained in the section above.

C. United States Constitution

The federal constitution is published in volume 1 of O.C.G.A. and the *West's Code of Georgia Annotated*. An index immediately follows the federal constitution. It is also available in print in the first few volumes of U.S.C.A. and U.S.C.S. Additionally, publications of other states' codes may include the U.S. Constitution, just as the Georgia codes do.

The federal constitution is widely available online. LexisNexis and Westlaw provide annotated versions.

D. Federal Court Rules

Rules similar to Georgia's court rules exist on the federal level. They are published in *Georgia Court Rules and Procedures—Federal* as well as in U.S.C., U.S.C.A., and U.S.C.S. Placement of the rules varies among the statutory publications. In U.S.C. and U.S.C.A., for example, the Federal Rules of Appellate Procedure appear just after title 28. In U.S.C.S., those rules are found at the end of all fifty titles in separate volumes devoted to rules.

As at the state level, each court may have its own "local rules" with specific practices required by that court. Check the annotated codes and West deskbooks or look on the court's website to learn about local rules. The U.S. Supreme Court's rules are on its website at www.supremecourtus.gov.

Appendix 4-A. Comparison of the Two Current Georgia Codes

	Official Code of Georgia Annotated-O.C.G.A.	*West's Code of Georgia Annotated*-Ga. Code Ann.
Official/Unofficial	Official	Unofficial
Number of Volumes	44	65
Citation	Title-chapter-section	Title-chapter-section
	Three-unit numbering system	Three-unit numbering system
	(Both codes have same citation systems)	(Both codes have same citation systems)
Supplementation	Annual pocket parts	Annual pocket parts
	Advance Legislative Service	Georgia Legislative Service
	Advance Annotation Service (new annotations only)	Interim Annotation Service (new annotations only)
Notes of Decisions	Decisions of Georgia state cases and federal cases arising in Georgia	Decisions of Georgia state cases and federal cases arising in Georgia
	Attorney General Opinions	Attorney General Opinions
		More comprehensive than O.C.G.A.
Notes Involving Constitutionality of Statute	Appear first in annotations	Included
Notes to Bar Opinions	Included	Not included
History Line to Georgia Laws	Included	Included
Historical Notes	Amendment notes for recent years only	Selective amendment notes
Uniform State Laws	Included	Included
Georgia Constitution	Included	Included
U.S. Constitution	Included	Included
Cross-references	Cross-references to related constitutional and statutory provisions	Cross-references to related constitutional and statutory provisions

Appendix 4-A. Comparison of the Two Current Georgia Codes, cont'd

	Official Code of Georgia Annotated-O.C.G.A.	*West's Code of Georgia Annotated*-Ga. Code Ann.
Administrative Code References	References to rules and regulations	References to rules and regulations
Law Review Citations	Georgia law reviews *Georgia Bar Journal*	Georgia law reviews Selective national law reviews
Library References to A.L.R., Am. Jur., C.J.S., and Other Resources	Included	Included and also West's key numbers Forms Georgia practice titles
Federal Laws	Not included	Cross-references to U.S.C.A.
U.S. Supreme Court References	Not included	Included
Tables of Comparative Citations	1933 Code to 1981 Code 1981 Code to 1933 Code Constitutional provisions *Georgia Laws* to O.C.G.A. Other tables	Not included
Indexes	Subject Index Short Title Index Index to Local & Special Laws since 1730 Each title has own index	Subject Index Popular Name Table Yearly Legislative Highlights Index Each title has own index
Online Availability	LexisNexis	Westlaw

Appendix 4-B. Online Sources for the Georgia Code

CASEMAKER—Free to members of the State Bar of Georgia www.gabar.org/casemaker	
Content	Unannotated Code
Coverage	Current
Update	Continuous

GEORGIA GENERAL ASSEMBLY—Free www.legis.state.ga.us (follow "Georgia Code" hyperlink)	
Content	Unannotated Code—text is O.C.G.A., provided by LexisNexis
Coverage	Current
Update	Continuous
Notes	Search by terms or code section

LEXISNEXIS—Commercial www.lexis.com	
Content	Annotated Code—O.C.G.A. only
Coverage	Current, Archive from 1991–present
Update	Continuous

LOISLAW—Commercial www.loislaw.com	
Content	Annotated Code—O.C.G.A. only
Coverage	Current, Archive from 1991–present
Update	Continuous

LOISLAW—Commercial www.loislaw.com	
Content	Unannotated Code—text is O.C.G.A.
Coverage	Current code with hyperlinks to current amendments
Update	Quarterly

WESTLAW—Commercial www.westlaw.com	
Content	O.C.G.A. (LexisNexis) and Ga. Code Ann. (West)
Coverage	O.C.G.A. (LexisNexis) 1988–present; Ga. Code Ann. (West) 2002–present
Update	Annually

Appendix 4-C. Online Sources for Georgia Session Laws

CASEMAKER — Free to members of the State Bar of Georgia www.gabar.org/casemaker	
Content	Session laws
Coverage	Current session
Update	Posted as they become available
GALILEO: GEORGIA LEGISLATIVE DOCUMENTS — Free www.galileo.usg.edu (available at Georgia educational institutions and public libraries)	
Content	Session laws — only online source of retrospective coverage
Coverage	1799–1999
Update	Plans to add more years
Notes	Search by subject or year and page number to *Georgia Laws*
GEORGIA GENERAL ASSEMBLY — Free www.legis.state.ga.us	
Content	Session laws in .pdf or .htm; lists sponsors
Coverage	1995–present
Update	Continuous during legislative session
Notes	Search by bill number, subject, or code section number; cannot locate law by session law number
LEXISNEXIS — Commercial www.lexis.com	
Content	Session laws
Coverage	1989–present
Update	Continuous during legislative session
LOISLAW — Commercial www.loislaw.com	
Content	Session laws
Coverage	1997–present
Update	Click on "Currency"
WESTLAW — Commercial www.westlaw.com	
Content	Session laws
Coverage	1990–present
Update	Continuous during legislative session

Appendix 4-D. Online Sources for the Georgia Constitution

CASEMAKER—Free to members of the State Bar of Georgia www.gabar.org/casemaker	
Content	Georgia Constitution without annotations
Coverage	Current constitution
Update	Ten days from electronic posting of change
GEORGIA SECRETARY OF STATE—Free www.sos.state.ga.us/elections/2003_constitution.pdf	
Content	Georgia Constitution without annotations in .pdf
Coverage	Revised 2005
Update	As revised
LEXISNEXIS—Commercial www.lexis.com	
Content	Georgia Constitution with annotations
Coverage	Current constitution
Update	Quarterly
LOISLAW—Commercial www.loislaw.com	
Content	Georgia Constitution without annotations
Coverage	Current constitution
Update	Click on "Currency"
WESTLAW—Commercial www.westlaw.com	
Content	Georgia Constitution with annotations
Coverage	Current constitution
Update	Check "Scope" information for currency

Appendix 4-E. Online Sources for Georgia Court Rules

CASEMAKER—Free to members of the State Bar of Georgia www.gabar.org/casemaker	
Content	All court rules
Coverage	Current
Update	Ten days from notice of change
GEORGIA COURT OF APPEALS—Free www.gaappeals.us	
Content	Rules of the Georgia Court of Appeals
Coverage	Current
Update	Yearly
Notes	No subject searching
GEORGIA SUPREME COURT—Free www.gasupreme.us	
Content	Rules and amendments for the Georgia Supreme Court
Coverage	Current
Update	Continuous
Notes	No subject searching
JUDICIAL BRANCH OF GEORGIA—Free www.georgiacourts.org/rules.html	
Content	Links to Rules of Supreme Court, Court of Appeals, Uniform Rules
Coverage	Dates vary; check individual court rules sites
Update	Varies
Notes	Can search entire site by subject
LEXISNEXIS—Commercial www.lexis.com	
Content	All court rules, case annotations, orders
Coverage	Current
Update	Two times per year, case annotations monthly
LOISLAW—Commercial www.loislaw.com	
Content	All court rules
Coverage	Current
Update	Click on "Currency"
WESTLAW—Commercial www.westlaw.com	
Content	All court rules, local rules from selected counties, orders
Coverage	Current
Update	Continuous

Chapter 5

Legislative History

After reading this chapter you will:
- understand Georgia's legislative process;
- be familiar with online and paper documents that are part of an act's legislative history;
- know the steps in completing a legislative history for a Georgia act; and
- be familiar with federal legislative history materials.

This chapter covers the process by which the Georgia General Assembly enacts laws. It begins with an overview of the legislative process in Georgia; through that process, the statutory laws of Georgia are enacted and changed. This chapter then describes the process of *bill tracking*, monitoring the status of a current bill that may or may not ultimately be enacted. Lawyers track bills that may affect a client's interests when they are acting in an advisory role.

Next, this chapter explains how to research the *legislative history* of a statute that has already been enacted. For most areas of law, courts apply the "plain meaning rule," which means that statutes are to be interpreted using the ordinary meaning of the language of the statute. In light of the plain meaning rule, Georgia makes use of the language of the act and the progress of the act through the legislative process, as disclosed by the *Journal of the House of Representatives* and the *Journal of the Senate* (1799–present) (hereinafter *Journals*). Researching legislative history for a Georgia act is very different from researching legislative history for a federal act. For Georgia acts, there are very few legislative documents to review, whereas, on the federal level, there are volumes of materials to review.

I. The Legislative Process

Reviewing the legislative process and the documents connected with the legislative process helps you understand how a bill becomes a law. The Georgia General Assembly consists of a House of Representatives and a Senate. The House is the larger of the two chambers with 180 members and is presided over by the Speaker of the House. The Senate has 56 members, and the Lieutenant Governor is the President of the Senate.

The annual legislative session begins the second Monday in January and lasts forty legislative days, usually adjourning in mid-March. Table 5-1 shows the basic progression of an idea from bill to statute and notes the documents that are important in legal research. These documents are explained later in the chapter.

Table 5-1. How a Bill Becomes a Law and Documents Attached to the Process

Process	Documents
An idea for legislation is suggested by a citizen, group, or legislator.	
Legislator works with the Office of Legislative Counsel. Counsel drafts the language of the bill.	
Legislator files the bill in either the House or Senate. Bills to raise money must be introduced in the House.	Bills are printed with bill number, identification code, bill authors, title, and text. The text of the bill, as introduced, is not printed in the *Journals*.
On the legislative day after filing, the bill is formally introduced. The bill's title is read for the first time and the bill is assigned to a committee.	First Readers, a record of the title of the bill that is read aloud once very quickly, are noted in *Journals*.
In the House only, the Clerk reads the bill's title for second time.	Second Readers are noted in *Journals*.
In the Senate, second reading comes after a bill is reported favorably from committee.	

Table 5-1. How a Bill Becomes a Law and
Documents Attached to the Process, cont'd

The committee considers the bill; author and other legislators may testify. If controversial, public hearings may be held.	Committee recommendation on each bill reported out of committee is noted in *Journals*.
If the bill is passed, it goes to the other chamber for the same treatment.	The engrossed bill is a proofread bill passed by one of the chambers.
Once the presiding officer calls a bill up from the Rules Calendar, the Clerk reads the bill's title (Third Reading). Bill goes to floor for debates and amendments.	Calendars are produced. Debates are not recorded or published by either chamber. Audio and video are available at www.georgia.gov. Amendments are printed in *Journals*.
After debate, members vote. If a bill is approved by a majority of the total membership of that chamber, it is sent to the other. (Very few bills require a super-majority.)	Voting on final passage is recorded in *Journals*. Legislators may enter statements in *Journals* as to why they voted in a particular way.
If the second chamber changes the bill, it is returned to the chamber where it was introduced. If changes are accepted, the bill is sent to the Governor. If the first chamber rejects changes and second chamber insists, a conference committee may be appointed (composed of members from each chamber; designed to reach a compromise version of the bill). If the committee report is accepted by both chambers, the bill is sent to the Governor.	
Bill is sent to the Governor. Otherwise, all enrolled bills sent to Governor following adjournment. After 40 days, bills become law.	The final version of the bill that is sent to the Governor is the enrolled bill.

Table 5-1. How a Bill Becomes a Law and Documents Attached to the Process, cont'd

Governor may sign bill or do nothing, and bill becomes law. Governor may veto bill; two-thirds of members of each house are required to override Governor's veto.	Vetoes and some reasons for vetoes are printed in the *Journals*.
The enacted bill is assigned an act number. The act becomes effective July 1 unless a different effective date is provided.	Acts, also called session laws, are printed in the *Georgia Laws* chronologically by act number.
The act is codified, meaning that it is arranged by topic in the code. It uses the code number that is in the original law.	Act is incorporated into the *Official Code of Georgia Annotated* and the *Georgia Code Annotated*.

An excellent book on Georgia legislative procedures and practices is the *Handbook for Georgia Legislators*.[1] This book covers the lawmaking process, rules of procedures, and legislative staff and resources. It is published by the Carl Vinson Institute of Government at the University of Georgia. You can find more information about the Carl Vinson Institute at www.cviog.uga.edu.

The General Assembly classifies bills under consideration as general, local, or special in their application. According to the Georgia Constitution, art. III, §6, para. 4(a), general laws have uniform operation throughout the state, and no local or special law may be passed in subject areas covered by a general law. Local acts, which make up a high percentage of the bills passed, apply to a specific city, county, or special district named in the act. A special law, although not currently enacted, affects a limited area or class.

---

1. Edwin L. Jackson, Mary E. Stakes, & Paul T. Hardy, *Handbook for Georgia Legislators* (13th ed. 2006). This book is available from the Carl Vinson Institute of Government at www.cviog.uga.edu.

Table 5-2. Outline for Bill Tracking Online

---

1. Go the legislature's website at www.legis.ga.gov.

2. Click on "Legislation."

3. When you know the bill number, fill the number in the box, e.g., SB 507.

4. When you do not know the bill number, do a text search by keyword or by code citation.

5. You will be sent to the status page (see Table 5-3 for an example).

II. Georgia Bill Tracking

A. Bill Tracking Online

Of the many bills that are introduced in each legislative session, some may affect the rights of a client by proposing new laws or amending existing laws. In advising a client, an attorney needs to learn of any bills on topics relevant to the client's interests and follow their progress through the process outlined above. Online bill tracking, rather than using the print materials, is the norm since the print materials are available only at the Georgia General Assembly. Keep in mind that the online version may include slightly different information from the print composite sheet. Table 5-2 gives an outline of the process for bill tracking online.

The Georgia General Assembly's website at www.legis.ga.gov is available at no charge. On this website, you can find information on committees, the full texts of bills and amendments, and information on representatives. The coverage for bills is 1995 to the present. The bill status information includes sponsors, detailed status history, First Reader summaries votes, and versions of the texts of the bills. You can search for bills by topic, bill number, and code number. The State Bar of Georgia at www.gabar.org also provides a tracking service during the legislative session.

Older bills are available in microform from the Clerk of the House (1979–present) and the Secretary of the Senate (1969–present). The

Table 5-3. Example of a Bill Status Page Online

Georgia General Assembly

Legislation | House | Senate | Information | Offices | Home

SB 507 - Ga. Smokefree Air Act; prohibit smoking in certain facilities/areas; penalties

(1) Thomas,Don 54th   (2) Reed,Kasim 35th   (3) Unterman,Renee 45th
(4) Thomas,Regina 2nd   (5) Lee,Daniel 29th   (6) Gillis,Hugh 20th

SC: H&HS   HC: GAff   03/12/04 - House Second Readers

First Reader Summary

A BILL to be entitled an Act to amend Chapter 12 of Title 16 of the Official Code of Georgia Annotated, relating to offenses against public health and morals, so as to enact the "Georgia Smokefree Air Act of 2004"; to prohibit smoking in certain facilities and areas; to state findings; to provide for definitions; to provide for exceptions; to provide for posting of signs; to provide for violations, penalties, and state and local government enforcement and administration; to provide for construction; to provide that this prohibition shall be cumulative to other general or local acts, rules, and regulations; to repeal a former prohibition against smoking in public places; to provide for related matters; to repeal conflicting laws; and for other purposes.

Electronically Recorded Votes

Date	Time	Vote No	Yeas	Nays	NV	Exc	Description
3/04/04	12:46 PM	Senate V0847	053	000	000	003	ADOPTION OF AMENDMENT #1 (AM 3
3/04/04	12:48 PM	Senate V0848	048	004	001	003	ADOPTION OF AMEND #3a BY SEN F
3/04/04	12:49 PM	Senate V0849	043	010	000	003	ADOPTION OF AMENDMENT #3 (AM 3
3/04/04	12:51 PM	Senate V0850	026	027	000	003	ADOPTION OF AMENDMENT #5 (AM 3
3/04/04	12:53 PM	Senate V0851	024	029	000	003	MOTION TO RECONSIDER AMENDMENT
3/04/04	12:55 PM	Senate V0852	045	007	001	003	PASSAGE BY SUBSTITUTE

Bill History

Date	Action
02/12/04	Senate Read and Referred
02/20/04	Senate Committee Favorably Reported
02/23/04	Senate Read Second Time

Georgia State Archives, which provides an online catalog available at www.georgiaarchives.org, is the only source for very old print bills beginning in 1838. Very old bills are not available online.

In addition to the General Assembly website, there are several excellent commercial websites for bill tracking. Table 5-4 lists the commercial bill tracking sites.

B. Bill Tracking Using Print Materials

Several print materials are available to the public during the legislative sessions. The print materials are available in person from the

Table 5-4. Commercial Sources of Georgia Bills and Bill Tracking Online

GEORGIA TRACK www.gatrack.com Online Legislation Tracking Service	
Content	Information about legislation and status of bills
Coverage	Subscriptions available for different levels—Individual, Professional, Agency/Corporation, Association
Update	Daily during legislative session
LEXISNEXIS www.lexis.com	
Content and Coverage	Full Text Bills (1995–present)
	Bill Tracking (current session only)
Update	Daily during legislative session
WESTLAW www.westlaw.com	
Content and Coverage	Full Text Bills (1991–present)
	Bill Tracking (2000–present)
	Legislative History Materials, including bill histories, amendments, daily reports, news releases, votes, press releases from Governor (date of coverage varies by source)
Update	Daily during legislative session

Table 5-5. General Assembly Materials

Name	Description
Calendars	Copies of the daily calendar of business for each chamber
First Readers	Measures that have been introduced and read only once (by title, with notation of committee referral)
Daily Status Sheet	A single-page listing of floor and committee action by both chambers
Composite Status Sheet	A multi-page consolidated listing of the status of all bills and resolutions introduced that session
Senate and House Bills and Resolutions	Bills are proposed legislation considered by the General Assembly. Resolutions are legislative proposals used to express the opinion or will of one or both houses. Resolutions are similar to bills, and may or may not have the force of law, depending on the subject matter.

General Assembly. All of the materials listed in Table 5-5, except for the Composite Status Sheet, are also available on the House and Senate websites and the General Assembly website. Sometimes the electronic version of information does not appear in exactly the same format as the printed version.

C. Georgia Public Television

Georgia Public Television (WGTV) provides television access to the legislative session. The program, *The Lawmakers*, airs on official legislative days during the session and includes coverage of the session, supplemented by interviews and analyses.[2] In addition, the Georgia General Assembly website provides live audio and video of gavel-to-gavel coverage of the Georgia General Assembly legislative session.[3]

---

2. Georgia Public Broadcasting, *The Lawmakers*, at www.gpb.org/public/tv/lawmakers provides Internet access to previously aired shows.
3. Georgia General Assembly, Live Broadcast, at www.legis.state.ga.us/legis.

III. Georgia Legislative History Research

Legislative history research is the reverse of bill tracking. Bill tracking follows the legislative process forward, from the introduction of a bill to its possible enactment. In contrast, legislative history research works backwards, beginning with an enacted statute.

A. Role of Georgia Courts

The courts in Georgia determine the meaning of a statute by referring to its actual language.[4] When construing statutory enactments, the courts must diligently look for the intention of the General Assembly in passing the law, "keeping in view at all times the old law, the evil, and the remedy."[5] The courts have ruled that determinations of the legislature's intent should come from the plain language of the statute.[6] Professor Sentell explains in his article, *Georgia Statutory Construction: The Use of Legislative History*, how the Georgia Supreme Court accepts the use of the term "legislative history" within a broad range of contexts.[7]

If anyone questions the interpretation of the meaning or the validity of any statute due to ambiguous wording, vagueness, uncertain legislative intent, conflicts with other laws, or questionable constitutionality, Georgia law imposes upon the courts sole responsibility for the construction of statutes.[8] Georgia courts have held that the testimony of members of the legislature — even the bill's author — is inadmissible to show legislative intent.[9]

There may be a question as to whether the act was enacted according to constitutional requirements. Under the enrolled bill rule

---

4. *Williamson v. Lucas*, 171 Ga. App. 695, 697 (1984).
5. O.C.G.A. § 1-3-1(a) (Supp. 2006).
6. *Bd. of Tr. v. Christy*, 246 Ga. App. 553, 554 (1980).
7. R. Perry Sentell, Jr., *Georgia Statutory Construction: The Use of Legislative History*, Ga. St. B.J., Apr. 1996, at 30.
8. *Modern Homes Constr. Co. v. Burke*, 219 Ga. 710 (1964).
9. *S. Ry. Co. v. A.O. Smith*, 134 Ga. App. 219 (1975).

in Georgia, the courts presume that a duly enrolled act, authenticated by the presiding officer of each chamber, approved by the Governor, and deposited with the Secretary of State, has been enacted according to constitutional requirements.[10] For example, the bill must be read on the floor of the General Assembly three times. If the title of the bill is literally not read on the floor, the bill would not have been enacted according to constitutional requirements.

B. Sources of Georgia Legislative History

Notwithstanding all the judicial arguments against investigating the extraneous matters surrounding the statute's passage, legislative history materials provide valuable insight into the genesis of the law.

1. Types of Legislative History Materials

As noted in Table 5-1, legislative history material in Georgia includes the following: versions of the bills, votes, and amendments to the bills printed in the *Journals*; session laws; and the codes (*Official Code of Georgia Annotated* and the *Georgia Code Annotated*). The unofficial source of legislative history includes the Review of Selected Georgia Legislation in the *Georgia State University Law Review*. Additionally, a Westlaw database titled "Georgia Legislative History" pieces together some of the other unofficial sources of legislative history, including news releases and press releases.

A researcher should begin with the codes in order to uncover the intent of the legislature. Each statute provides citations to the *Georgia Laws* that created or amended the statute. You can find a discussion of *Georgia Laws* in Chapter 4 of this book. Compilers of the *Georgia Laws* write the preamble or caption "solely to assist the reader in quickly determining the subject matter" of an act. However, when the General Assembly enacts the act, these captions do not constitute part of the act. These preambles may prove useful in determining intent. For example, such statements will read, "To amend O.C.G.A. re-

---

10. *Battallia v. Columbus*, 199 Ga. App. 897 (1991).

lating to insurance generally, so as to change the definition of insurable interest...." The original bill, with its amendments, may provide insight into the intent of the legislative body. These preambles are not codified, so you must refer to *Georgia Laws* for the preambles.

In Georgia, the *Journals* are the sole official records of the proceedings of each house.[11] Each *Journal* includes the authors of every measure considered by the House or Senate, the dates of the readings of the measure, the name and date of committee assignments, and the committee recommendation on each bill or resolution reported out of the committee. Researchers can review events that occurred during the progress of a statute's enactment, as revealed by the *Journals*, in their search to find the intent of the legislature.[12]

The *Journals* do not contain the text of bills and resolutions; however, they include the committee or floor amendments and substitutes to a measure. The *Journals* report votes on all motions and on the final passage of bills or resolutions. Though the *Journals* do not include individual floor remarks and debates, the Georgia courts may review events occurring during the progress of a bill as recorded by the *Journals*.[13] When a roll call vote is utilized, the names of all members and their votes are recorded.

The legislative committees remain active throughout the session. Although both legislative and conference committees are involved in the legislative process and make reports to the House and Senate, they do not publish their reports, except by noting them in the *Journals*. These single sentences state that the committee has considered the legislation and recommends that the legislation pass as introduced, pass as modified, or not pass. Unfortunately, the legislature does not transcribe the floor debates, nor does it issue written legislative committee reports. Other types of committees include study committees, ad hoc committees, and interim committees, which study proposed new legislation. The House and Senate websites at

---

11. Ga. Const. art. III, §5, para. 1.
12. *Sharpe v. Lowe*, 214 Ga. 513, 518 (1958).
13. *Id.*

www.legis.state.ga.us/legis include valuable information on committees. Study committee reports and ad hoc committee reports may
also be obtained from either the House Clerk's Office or the Secretary of the Senate.

Therefore, in Georgia, although there are the *Journals*, the information in the *Journals* is of limited value since the committee reports
are merely one sentence. The *Journals* are valuable for printing
amendments to the bills, although they do not print the original bill.
Hence, possibly the most accessible sources of legislative intent are
the bills and amendments themselves. The researcher would compare
the various versions of the bills throughout the legislative session.

2. Unofficial Sources for Georgia Legislative History

A popular source of legislative history materials is the Review of
Selected Georgia Legislation in the *Georgia State University Law Review*.[14] These reviews, known as the Peach Sheets, began in 1985 and
present well-documented histories of Georgia legislation. Not every
bill has a Peach Sheet written about it. Due to limited resources (time
and student authors), editors select laws based on how significant the
legislation will be in terms of changes to existing laws.

The research in the Peach Sheets includes an analysis of the reasons for the bill's introduction, the pressures on the bill during its
course through the legislature, and the public perceptions at the time
the legislature was considering the bill. To gather this information,
law review students conduct research through personal interviews,
analysis of prior statutory and case law, identification of the various
changes the bill went through during the legislative process, and
identification of public perceptions as revealed by newspaper ac-
counts of the legislative activity. Additionally, student authors listen
to the entire floor debate for the bill covered. The authors then transcribe and incorporate the relevant portions of the debate into the
Peach Sheet to see what substantive revisions were made.

---

14. Georgia State University Law Review, Peach Sheets, at http://law.gsu
.edu/lawreview/peachsheets.htm (online 2000–present).

Table 5-6. Westlaw's Georgia Legislative History Database

WESTLAW www.westlaw.com	
Content and Coverage	Full Text Bills (1991–present)
	Bill Tracking (2000–present)
	Legislative History Materials, including bill histories, amendments, daily reports, news releases, votes, and press releases from the Governor (dates of coverage vary by source, but not before 2000)
Update	Daily during legislative session

Another source of legislative history materials is the Annual Survey of Georgia Law in the *Mercer Law Review*.[15] The survey, published since 1950, includes articles discussing legislative issues.

In addition, there is an excellent database on Westlaw that aids the researcher with piecing together the bills, amendments, and other information. This database is unique in that it combines official and unofficial information on individual bills in one database. Table 5-6 outlines the features of this noteworthy database, Georgia Legislative History.

C. Locating Legislative History Sources in Print and Online

Before beginning legislative history research, you must know the codified number of the statute that you need to research. Review Chapter 4 on researching Georgia statutes, if necessary. At the end of each statute in the *Official Code of Georgia Annotated* (O.C.G.A.) and *West's Code of Georgia Annotated* (Ga. Code Ann.), is a note that gives the history of the statute. This note includes a reference to the session law that was codified as this statute and the date of enactment.

---

15. Recent issues of the *Mercer Law Review* are available at www.law .mercer.edu/academics/lawreview/index.cfm.

To find the legislative documents that contain Georgia legislative history, follow the steps below.

1. Start with the O.C.G.A. or Ga. Code Ann. Beginning with the code citation, find the session law number that includes the date of enactment, e.g., Ga. L. 2004, Act 720, § 1. Remember, this history information can be found following the text of the statutes in the codes. See Table 5-7.

2. Read the *Georgia Laws*. These are the session laws for Georgia. Carefully read the language of the act, noting the caption or preamble written solely by the compilers of *Georgia Laws* to assist you in quickly determining the subject matter of the act. Also, note the House or Senate bill number. See Table 5-8.

3. Check for amendments to the bill as listed on the Georgia General Assembly website or in the printed *Journals*. The amendments may give you insight into the legislative intent of the bill. See Table 5-9.

4. Consult *Georgia State University Law Review* Peach Sheets for the year that the bill was passed into law. In the example above, the bill was passed in 2004 and it was Act 720. The Peach Sheets has the act indexed under "Education." See Table 5-10.

5. Check the Georgia Legislative Materials database on Westlaw, the General Assembly website, or other commercial databases. See Table 5-11.

6. Finding cases and secondary materials may give you some insight. Cases and secondary materials are explained in other chapters of this book.

Table 5-7. Excerpt from Georgia Code on Westlaw

(c)(1) Prior to May 1, 2007, each school system shall adopt the following reporting system for purposes of identifying and qualifying graduating seniors for the HOPE scholarship program and other programs identified in this Code section:

  (A) A final grade average of at least an 80 numeric average in their core curriculum subjects, provided that the student meets the college preparatory curriculum requirements; or
  (B) A final grade average of at least an 85 numeric average in their core curriculum subjects if the student meets the career/technical curriculum requirements.
  (2) Prior to May 1, 2007, only the reporting system as indicated in this subsection shall be used to determine eligibility for all grants, scholarships, or loans to attend colleges or universities which are administered pursuant to Article 7 of Chapter 3 of this title and eligibility for enrollment in postsecondary courses pursuant to Code Section 20-2-161.1.

Laws 1994, p. 1057, § 1; Laws 1998, p. 626, § 1; Laws 2004, Act 720, § 1, eff. July 1, 2004.

Reprinted from Westlaw with permission of Thomson/West.

Table 5-8. Excerpt from *Georgia Laws*

House Bill 1325 (AS PASSED HOUSE AND SENATE)

By: Representatives McBee of the 74th, Purcell of the 122nd, Greene of the 134th, Holmes of the 48th, Post 1, and Cummings of the 19th

A BILL TO BE ENTITLED
AN ACT

To amend Chapters 2 and 3 of Title 20 of the Official Code of Georgia Annotated, relating to elementary and secondary education and to postsecondary education, respectively, so as to change the reporting system and method for determining eligibility for HOPE scholarships, other scholarships, grants, or loan assistance, and certain postsecondary courses and advanced placement courses for students enrolling as freshmen in eligible public or private postsecondary institutions on or after May 1, 2007; to add public and private schools accredited by the Southern Association of Independent Schools to the definition of eligible high schools for the purposes of the HOPE program; to delete an obsolete reference; to revise and add definitions; to provide for loss of eligibility for the HOPE scholarship for any student who does not possess at least a cumulative 3.0 grade point average at the end of each spring quarter or semester; to provide for loss of eligibility for the HOPE scholarship for any part-time students under certain conditions; to provide for restoration of such eligibility; to provide for courses taken as postsecondary options to be included in HOPE hour limits; to provide for a set amount for mandatory fees for HOPE scholarships and HOPE grants; to provide for changes to the amount of HOPE scholarships at private institutions for students enrolled less than full-time; to provide for a limitation on quarter hours or semester hours of eligibility for HOPE grants and eligibility for combined HOPE scholarships and grants; to provide for exceptions; to create the HOPE Scholarship/Pre-K Legislative Oversight Committee; to provide for membership and duties of such oversight committee; to provide that employees of certain organizations are considered residents of Georgia for purposes of the HOPE program; to amend Code Section 50-27-13 of the Official Code of Georgia Annotated, relating to disposition of lottery proceeds, budget report by Governor, appropriations by General Assembly, and shortfall reserve subaccount, so as to provide for changes to the amount of book allowances and fees for a HOPE scholarship or grant under certain conditions; to provide for related matters; to repeal conflicting laws; and for other purposes.

Table 5-9. Excerpt from General Assembly Website

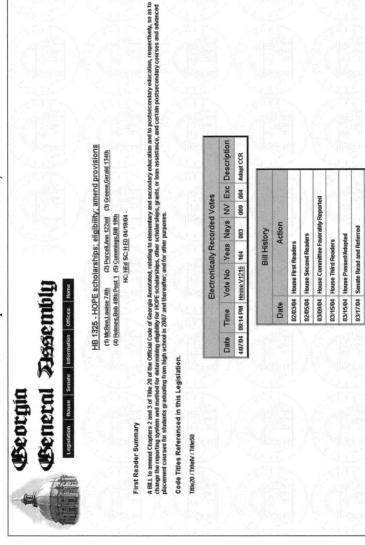

Table 5-10. Excerpt from Peach Sheet

GEORGIA STATE UNIVERSITY LAW REVIEW

VOLUME 21	NUMBER 1	FALL 2004

EDUCATION

Elementary and Secondary Education and Postsecondary Education: Change the Reporting System and Method for Determining Eligibility for HOPE Scholarships, Other Scholarships, Grants or Loan Assistance and for Postsecondary Courses and Advanced Placement Courses for Students Enrolling as Freshmen in Eligible Public or Private Postsecondary Institutions on or After May 1, 2007

Elizabeth Ballard & Emily Pittman

CODE SECTIONS:	O.C.G.A. §§ 20-2-157, 20-3-519 to -519.5 (amended), -519.13 to -519.14 (new), 50-27-13 (amended)
BILL NUMBER:	SB 471, HB 1325
ACT NUMBER:	720
GEORGIA LAWS:	2004 Ga. Laws 922
SUMMARY:	The Act amends existing Georgia law relating to the following: (1) the eligibility requirements for HOPE scholarships and grants; (2) the residency requirements for HOPE scholarships and grants; (3) the Scholarship's amount as it pertains to fees and books; (4) the hours of eligibility for HOPE grants; (5) the maintenance of a 3.0 grade point average at the end of each spring quarter or semester; and (6) the creation of the Lottery for Education Legislative Oversight Committee to protect the future of HOPE scholarships and grants.
EFFECTIVE DATE:	July 1, 2004

Introduction

Legislators introduced HB 1325 and SB 471, which were similar bills, in the 2004 legislative session to secure and protect the future of Georgia's Helping Outstanding Pupils Educationally ("HOPE") Scholarship.[1] However, a bipartisan Conference Committee was necessary to resolve differences between the bills.[2] The Conference Committee amended and adopted HB 1325 to establish the new legislation.[3] The *History* section of this legislative review discusses the history of the HOPE Scholarship. The *Bill Tracking* section discusses SB 471 and HB 1325 and their similarities and differences, as well as the Conference Committee amendments

This work was originally published with the *Georgia State University Law Review.*
The original text can be found at 21 Ga. St. U. L. Rev. 107 (2004–05).

Table 5-11. Excerpt from Westlaw

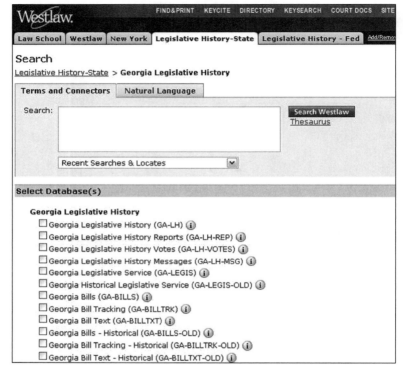

Reprinted from Westlaw with permission of Thomson/West.

IV. Federal Legislative Research

A. Federal Bill Tracking

Bill tracking for federal legislation is best accomplished using on-line sources. More Congressional material is available daily on the Internet, and using Internet sources for bill tracking is often easier than using print sources. The Library of Congress website at http://thomas.loc.gov provides bill summaries and status, committee reports, selected hearings, and debates. The U.S. Government Printing Office site at www.access.gpo.gov contains bills, bill status, reports, selected hearings, and debates. Coverage varies even within a single website, so check carefully. Westlaw and LexisNexis also have excellent databases for federal bill tracking.

B. Federal Legislative History

Researching federal legislative history is very different from researching Georgia laws due to the wealth of legislative documents that are available. There are many different types of documents that provide insight to the legislative process of a bill. For example, federal materials on bills include extensive reports, along with transcripts of committee hearings, and long debates on the floor of Congress. Whereas, in Georgia, the reports are just one sentence in the *Journals*, and there are no transcripts of committee hearings or recorded debates on the floor of the General Assembly.

Bills are numbered sequentially in each chamber of Congress. Generally, Senate bill numbers are preceded by an "S," and House bill numbers are preceded by "H.R." When a federal statute is enacted, it is printed as a small booklet and assigned a public law number. This number is in the form "Pub. L. No. 101-336," where the numerals before the hyphen are the number of the Congress in which the law was enacted and the numerals after the hyphen are assigned chronologically as bills are enacted. The public law number given above is for the Americans with Disabilities Act (ADA), which was passed in 1990 during the 101st Congress.

The new statute is later published as a session law in *United States Statutes at Large*, which is the federal counterpart of *Georgia Laws*. Session laws are designated by volume and page in *Statutes at Large*, e.g., 104 Stat. 328. Finally, the new statute is assigned a statute number when it is codified with statutes on similar topics in the *United States Code*. The citation for the first section of the ADA is 42 U.S.C. § 12101.

As with Georgia legislative history, you must begin federal legislative history research with a statute number. If you do not know the statute number, use an annotated code to find it (as described in Chapter 4). With a statute number, you can find the session law citation and public law number, which will lead to the legislative history of the bill as it worked its way through Congress.

1. Sources of Federal Legislative History

In conducting federal legislative history research, you are looking for committee reports, materials from committee hearings, and transcripts of floor debates. Committee reports are considered the most persuasive authority. Congressional committee reports are often lengthy documents published in soft-cover format. These reports contain the committee's analysis of the bill, the reasons for enacting it, and the views of any members who disagree with those reasons. Congressional hearing materials include transcripts from the proceedings as well as documents such as prepared testimony and exhibits.

Floor debates are published in the *Congressional Record*. Floor debates are usually the least persuasive materials; however, debates may be important if the sponsor of the bill is debating the merits of the bill.

2. Compiled Legislative History

It will save you considerable time if you first check to see if a legislative history has been compiled. Check Nancy P. Johnson, *Sources of Compiled Legislative Histories*[16] either in print or on HeinOnline. This bibliography provides citations to compiled legislative histories. Compiled legislative histories include documents and other helpful citations to reports, hearings, and debates. A compiled legislative history can save a researcher hours of time hunting for these documents. Additionally, HeinOnline includes "The Legislative History Title Collection," which is a collection of full-text legislative histories on some of the most important and historically significant legislation of our time.

---

16. Nancy P. Johnson, *Sources of Compiled Legislative Histories: A Bibliography of Government Documents, Periodical Articles, and Books* (AALL 1979–present). Also available at www.heinonline.org.

3. Print Sources for Federal Legislative History

The *United States Code Congressional and Administrative News* (USCCAN) contains information from 1944 to the present. USCCAN includes the text of the law and at least one committee report as well as references to other reports and to the *Congressional Record*. Oftentimes, researchers use this set for a quick review of the law and the committee report. The set does not include all the documents necessary for a thorough review of the legislative history, but it does provide the committee report, which is often the best source of legislative intent. USCCAN is available on Westlaw.

4. Online Sources for Federal Legislative History

There are several excellent sources for conducting federal legislative history research online. The websites noted earlier in this chapter for tracking federal legislation also provide useful information for legislative history research. Thomas, the Library of Congress website at http://thomas.loc.gov, provides bills and bill status, public laws, committee reports, debates, and selected hearings. The U.S. Government Printing Office website at www.access.gpo.gov also contains bills and bill status, public laws, committee reports, debates, and selected hearings. The years covered vary on the two government sites, so you should check both. Westlaw and LexisNexis also have excellent databases for legislative history materials. In addition to the databases included in the LexisNexis legal system, the "LexisNexis Congressional" service is available through a subscription. It is a very extensive database for online federal legislative materials.

Chapter 6

Administrative Law

After reading this chapter you will:

- be familiar with steps for Georgia administrative research;
- understand the difference between Georgia agency sources such as rules and decisions and be able to locate them;
- be familiar with steps for federal administrative research;
- recognize the basic functions of and documents from state and federal administrative branches that mirror one another; and
- recognize that the agency itself may sometimes be the best source of information.

I. Introduction to Administrative Law and Governmental Agencies

Governmental agencies are created by enabling statutes tailored by the legislature to carry out functions of government not typically administered by the legislature. For example, the legislature may enact laws that assign the length of incarceration for different classes of convicted criminals, but not laws that govern what kind of clothing or hygiene habits are expected of inmates. The rules governing inmate behavior are created by governmental agencies.

Each enabling statute carefully defines the scope of the agency's power but typically includes rulemaking (legislative power), administrative adjudication (judicial power), and the collection and maintenance of information (executive power). Georgia governmental agencies function within the bounds of the Georgia Administrative

Table 6-1. Outline for Georgia Administrative Law Research

1. Find the statutory or constitutional provision granting the agency power to act. For assistance with constitutional or statutory research, refer to Chapter 4.

2. Research case law to determine whether the agency acted within that power. For assistance with case law research, refer to Chapters 2 and 3.

3. Find the text of the relevant administrative rule(s) in *Official Compilation Rules and Regulations of the State of Georgia.* Update the rules.

4. Find agency and judicial decisions applying the rule in similar circumstances. Update the decisions.

5. Research other administrative law resources if applicable.

Procedure Act[1] (A.P.A.) and mirror the three branches of the federal government in both form and function. Administrative law is the law created by administrative agencies and is considered primary source material.

Consider the following hypothetical as you read this chapter. Suppose you are an attorney who represents a male inmate in a state prison who has been asked to cut his long hair shorter. The inmate objects, so he hires you. As his attorney you will follow the steps for Georgia administrative law research in Table 6-1 to perform thorough research.

II. Administrative Rules

Administrative agencies promulgate *rules*, similar to the legislature enacting statutes. Administrative rules are written in a format simi-

---

1. O.C.G.A. §§ 50-13-1 to 50-13-42 (2006).

lar to statutes. While statutes are intentionally broad, agency rules are intentionally detailed. This detail by agency experts reflects the legislatively enabled power given to the agency. Think of the legislature as the generalist in policymaking, and think of the agency as a specialist in carrying out the details of the policy.

Often, courts seek guidance and expertise from the agency.[2] Rules can provide guidance about an agency's understanding of a statute. Although rules and statutes are both primary authority, rules are subordinate to statutes. Where there is a conflict or inconsistency between a rule and a statute, the statute wins.[3] Moreover, a rule cannot "cure" a statute that a court has held unconstitutional. Table 6-2 provides an example of a Georgia regulation that relates to the inmate hypothetical above. Compare the outcome of this hypothetical case if the inmate were in a federal prison by examining a similar federal regulation in Table 6-7.

A. Researching the Enabling Act

Analytically, the initial question is whether the agency acted within its power. If that is in doubt, your first step in researching an administrative rule is to find the statute (or the constitutional provision) that gives the agency power to act. In Table 6-2, the enabling acts are the string of citations following the word "Authority" and ending just before the word "History" in the bottom paragraph.

---

2. "The administrative interpretation of a statute by an administrative agency which has the duty of enforcing or administering it is to be given great weight." *Mason v. Serv. Loan & Fin. Co.*, 128 Ga. App. 828, 831 (1973).
3. "The interpretation of a statute by the agency charged with enforcing or administering its provisions is to be given great weight and deference, unless contrary to law." *City of Atlanta v. Sumlin*, 258 Ga. App. 643, 645 (2002); *Smith v. Mr. Sweeper Stores*, 247 Ga. App. 726, 729 (2001). "[W]here the language of an Act is plain and unequivocal, judicial [or administrative] construction is not only unnecessary but is forbidden." *Chattahoochee Valley Home Health Care, Inc. v. Healthmaster, Inc.*, 191 Ga. App. 42, 44 (1989), quoting *City of Jesup v. Bennett*, 226 Ga. 606, 609 (1970).

Table 6-2. Example of a Georgia Agency Rule

```
125-2-3.04(6) Personal Hygiene [Inmates].
```

(6) Barber shops shall be maintained in accordance with standards established by the Department of Public Health or County Board of Health, as applicable. Each inmate shall have a conventional haircut. Hair shall not be longer than three (3) inches; shall not extend beyond a point which would reach the collar on an ordinary shirt; and shall not cover any part of the ears or eyebrows. Inmates may wear sideburns no longer than a point even with the bottom of the ear canal. Mustaches are permitted, but shall not extend beyond the edge of the mouth and must be kept neat and trimmed at all times. Goatees, beards, and similar facial adornments are prohibited, unless medically indicated.

Authority: Ga. Constitution 1982, 1983, Art. XI, Sec. I, O.C.G.A. Secs. 42-2-11, 42-5-53, 42-5-55, 42-10-2. History. Rule entitled "Personal Hygiene" adopted as R. 415-2-3-.04. F. Nov. 14, 1984; eff. Dec. 4, 1984, renumbered as R. 125-2-3-.04 of same title. F. June 28, 1985; eff. July 20, 1985, as specified by the Agency. Amended: F. Feb. 17, 1986; eff. Mar. 9, 1986. Amended: F. July 13, 1998; eff. Aug. 2, 1998. Amended: F. Feb. 6, 2003; eff. Feb. 26, 2003.

The next step is to find cases that interpret those provisions. This research will help determine whether the agency acted within the limits of its power in the situation that affects your client. Chapter 4 explains the process of searching the *Official Code of Georgia Annotated* (O.C.G.A.) and *West's Code of Georgia Annotated* (Ga. Code Ann.) to find constitutional provisions and statutes; the annotations in the O.C.G.A. and the Ga. Code Ann. provide references to relevant cases. Chapters 2 and 3 explain how to find additional cases using reporters, digests, and online sources. If the agency's power is clear, skip this inquiry and move directly to finding relevant rules, as explained next.

B. Locating Rules

The Secretary of State compiles, indexes, and publishes rules[4] issued by agencies and boards in Georgia in the multi-volume looseleaf set, *Official Compilation Rules and Regulations of the State of Georgia*. Rules are cited as, for example, Ga. Comp. R. & Regs. r. 125-2-3.04 (2003).

This set does not include rules from each agency because the Georgia A.P.A. outlines express exemptions from the statutory definition of "agency."[5] Exempted agencies have no rulemaking power. Some examples of exempted agencies are the Georgia General Assembly, the judiciary, the Governor, the State Board of Pardons and Paroles, the Board of Bar Examiners, the Board of Corrections, and the Department of Administrative Services. Consequently, the agency may be the only source of some rules.

The Office of the Secretary of State updates the *Official Compilation* upon receipt of changes from agencies and releases the updates to subscribers on a monthly basis. The *Official Compilation* arranges the rules alphabetically by agency, with each agency assigned a chapter number. In the example above, the number "125" is the chapter number, and it represents the Georgia Board of Corrections.

There is no current index to the *Official Compilation*. Therefore, you must either browse the chapter in question or use the Secretary of State's website at http://rules.sos.state.ga.us to search the table of contents of the *Official Compilation*. Although this website includes the full text of the rules, you should be aware that a search performed on this website is a search of the table of contents and not a search of the full text. You can search the full text of the rules on LexisNexis or Westlaw.

---

4. "'Rule' means each agency regulation, standard, or statement of general applicability that implements, interprets, or prescribes law or policy or describes the organization, procedure, or practice requirements of any agency." O.C.G.A. § 50-13-2(6) (2006).

5. O.C.G.A. § 50-13-2(1) (2006).

To learn more about the history of each rule, including identifying the filing, amendment, or repeal of each rule, consult the history line immediately following the text of the rule. In Table 6-2, the history line is in the bottom paragraph beginning with the word History.

To update a Georgia rule, use Loislaw's GlobalCite which locates cases and other resources within Loislaw that have cited a rule. You can also use the rule number as a search term on LexisNexis and Westlaw to find cases that cite the rule. Note that Shepard's and KeyCite do not support updating of state-level rules. See Chapter 7 for more information about updating.

There are additional resources available to monitor changes in Georgia rules. The *Georgia Government Register*, a LexisNexis service, is a companion to the *Official Compilation* and is available in print and online. The *Register*, available monthly since May 2001, is a tracking tool for rulemaking activity in Georgia. The publication includes emergency regulations, notices of proposed rulemaking, notification of modifications to existing Georgia regulations, certification pages of recent rulemaking activity, and other regulatory agency actions from selected Georgia agencies. The *Register* also includes an annual cumulative index.

Westlaw's "Georgia Regulation Tracking" database also provides tracking information for proposed and recently adopted Georgia rules. It includes a summary of the rule, the status, a citation, the sponsoring agency, and other administrative register information. LexisNexis also has a similar database called "Georgia State Regulation Tracking." It includes the same information as Westlaw's "Georgia Regulation Tracking," but the coverage extends to the most recent two years.

Table 6-3 provides information about online sources for rules of Georgia administrative agencies.

III. Researching Agency Decisions

In addition to their rulemaking function, agencies also act in a quasi-judicial role, adjudicating cases pertaining to agency rules or

Table 6-3. Online Sources of Agency Rules

Source Name	Web Address	Free or Commercial
Casemaker	www.gabar.org/casemaker	Free to members of the State Bar of Georgia
Georgia Secretary of State	www.sos.state.ga.us/rules_regs.htm	Free
Georgia.gov: Online Access to Georgia Government	www.georgia.gov	Free
LexisNexis	www.lexis.com	Commercial
Loislaw	www.loislaw.com	Commercial
Westlaw	www.westlaw.com	Commercial

actions and issuing opinions. For our inmate hypothetical, you will want to explore whether any opinions by the Georgia Board of Corrections are relevant.

There may be several levels of review depending on the agency. Typically, the first level may involve a reviewer or adjudicator considering the claimant's file and making a recommendation or determination. Subsequently, a hearing may be held before an Administrative Law Judge (ALJ); these proceedings may resemble short, informal trials.

The Georgia A.P.A. requires each agency to render decisions in contested cases. Check with the particular agency to learn the specific procedure it follows. Often, agency websites are a good source of procedural information. All of Georgia's agencies are accessible from Georgia's official website at www.georgia.gov. Although the Georgia Department of Corrections explains its internal grievance procedures on its website at www.dcor.state.ga.us/Divisions/Corrections/InmateAffairs.html, that department does not make the opinions of these internal bodies readily available on its website or through fee-based databases. Therefore, direct contact with the Georgia Department of Corrections is the best source of that agency's decisions.

In compliance with the Georgia A.P.A., agencies must maintain a publicly available file of decisions that contain findings of fact, rulings, final orders, and opinions.[6] However, in reality, except for the opinions of the Georgia Attorney General, agencies publish few administrative decisions, and many agencies do not report administrative decisions at all.

To obtain a copy of a decision written in the last thirty days, you must request it from the Office of State Administrative Hearings (OSAH). OSAH receives case referrals from "covered agencies," or agencies required to refer cases to OSAH for the initial hearing. After the ALJ conducts an initial hearing, OSAH keeps the records for the thirty-day appeal period.

After the thirty-day appeal period is over, OSAH releases the decision to the agency. The decisions are state records and accessible through an open records request. The Georgia Open Records Act opens all public records to inspection unless closed by a specific exception.[7]

The issuing agency is often the best, if not the only, source to obtain a paper copy of a decision. Few agencies make the full text of decisions available on their websites. Some vendors make the full text of selected agency opinions available online. Absent a comprehensive index to state administrative decisions, you may not know if relevant decisions exist. Therefore, using the few full-text, fee-based databases made available by vendors benefits researchers who seek administrative opinions. A list of online sources of selective agency decisions is provided in Table 6-4.

Table 6-4. Online Sources of Selective Agency Decisions

Source Name	Web Address	Free or Commercial
Georgia Department of Education	www.doe.k12.ga.us (click on "Appeals and Decisions")	Free
LexisNexis	www.lexis.com	Commercial
Westlaw	www.westlaw.com	Commercial

6. O.C.G.A. §§ 50-13-3 to 50-13-13 (2006).
7. O.C.G.A. §§ 50-18-70 to 50-18-135 (2006).

IV. Researching Attorney General Opinions

Under the Georgia Constitution, the Georgia Attorney General acts as the legal advisor of the executive branch, represents the state in the Supreme Court of Georgia in all capital felonies, and, when required by the Governor, represents the state in all civil and criminal cases.[8] Upon request of the Governor, the Attorney General issues opinions on "any question of law connected with the interest of the state or with the duties of any of the departments."[9] In 1978, the Attorney General stated that his opinions do not have the force and effect of court decisions.[10] But the recipient must adhere to these opinions unless a conflicting judicial decision reverses them or a legislative action makes them inapplicable. In Georgia courts, opinions of the Georgia Attorney General are persuasive authority but not binding.[11]

The Attorney General issues both official and unofficial opinions. Opinions rendered to the Governor or to heads of state departments are designated "official" opinions. The last two digits of the year serve as the serial numbers for the official opinions, which also include a chronological number, so the citation appears as 1990 Op. Ga. Att'y Gen. No. 90-2. Other officials provide unofficial opinions, which are informational only and do not bind the Attorney General or anyone else, for questions involving the general laws of the state. The letter "U" precedes the unofficial opinion numbers, for example, Op. Ga. Att'y Gen. No. U85-24.

The earliest published opinions of the Georgia Attorney General appeared in 1878, although the Attorney General has recorded opinions since 1875.[12] The set entitled *Opinions of the Attorney General* bound the opinions annually until it ceased publication in 1999. You can locate Georgia Attorney General Opinions in print through the multi-year *Tables and Index to the Opinions of the Attorney General* or

---

8. Ga. Const. art. V, § 3, para. 4.

9. O.C.G.A. § 45-15-3(1) (2002).

10. 1978 Op. Ga. Att'y Gen. No. 78-32.

11. Arthur Bolton, *The Attorney General of Georgia* 5–6 (1979).

12. Leah F. Chanin & Suzanne L. Cassidy, *Guide to Georgia Legal Research and Legal History* 189–92 (1990, supp. 1997).

Table 6-5. Online Sources of Attorney General Opinions

Source Name	Web Address	Free or Commercial
Casemaker	www.gabar.org/ casemaker	Free to members of the State Bar of Georgia
LexisNexis	www.lexis.com	Commercial
Office of the Attorney General of Georgia	www.ganet.org/ago/ opinions.html	Free
Westlaw	www.westlaw.com	Commercial

in the index to each volume of opinions. The annotated statutory codes cite official and unofficial Attorney General Opinions where appropriate. Table 6-5 lists online sources that include the full text of the Georgia Attorney General Opinions.

V. Researching Governor Executive Orders and Proclamations

The Governor has the power to issue executive orders that may support or enforce existing legislation, create commissions whose recommendations may result in new legislation, or otherwise influence the legislative process.[13] Since May 2001, the *Georgia Government Register* has provided print copies of executive orders. Table 6-6 lists sources of online access to executive orders and proclamations.

VI. Other Resources for Researching Georgia Administrative Law

The most valuable resource in administrative law research is the agency itself. While statutes and rules are relatively easy to find, you should be aware that additional policies, regulations, guidelines, and decisions exist that may be difficult to access. A large part of your re-

---

13. Ga. Const. art. V, §2, para. 1.

Table 6-6. Online Sources of Governor Executive Orders and
Proclamations

Source Name	Web Address	Coverage	Free or Commercial
Georgia Government Register (via LexisNexis)	www.lexis.com	Executive Orders	Commercial
Governor of Georgia	www.gov.state.ga.us	Executive Orders Proclamations	Free

search should be talking to the agency's representatives to find out
what material is available. In our inmate hypothetical, Attorney General
Opinions and Governor's Executive Orders and Proclamations
will, most likely, not be relevant. The Georgia Department of Corrections,
however, is a potential resource for locating relevant administrative
documents unique to that agency.

VII. Federal Administrative Law

The federal government's agencies function much like Georgia's.
Agencies such as the Department of Justice, the Internal Revenue Service,
and the U.S. Fish and Wildlife Service are invaluable parts of the
executive branch.

The federal A.P.A. is codified at 5 U.S.C. § 551 *et seq.* Like Georgia's
A.P.A., its goal is to promote uniformity, public participation,
and public confidence in the fairness of the procedures used by agencies
of the federal government.

A. *Code of Federal Regulations*

Federal administrative rules are called *regulations.* Federal regulations
are published in the *Code of Federal Regulations* (C.F.R.), which
is published by the U.S. Government Printing Office (G.P.O.) The
C.F.R. is a codification of regulations issued by federal agencies. Similar
to the *Official Compilation Rules and Regulations of the State of*

Georgia, federal regulations in C.F.R. are organized by agency and subject. The fifty titles of C.F.R. do not necessarily correspond to the fifty titles of the *United States Code* (U.S.C.), although some topics do fall under the same title number. For instance, title 7 in both C.F.R. and U.S.C. pertain to agriculture, while title 11 of U.S.C. addresses bankruptcy and the same title in C.F.R. deals with federal elections. See Table 6-7 for an example of federal regulations.

C.F.R. volumes are updated annually, with specific titles updated each quarter. Titles 1 through 16 are updated as of January 1; titles 17 through 27 are updated as of April 1; titles 28 through 41 are updated as of July 1; and titles 42 through 50 are updated as of October 1. Realize, though, that the updates may only become available months after the schedule indicates. Each year, the covers of C.F.R. volumes are a different color, which makes it easy to tell whether a print volume has been updated. If no changes were made in a particular volume for the new year, a cover with the new color is pasted on the old volume. (Title 3, "the president," is the exception to the publication schedule described above. A new volume is always published annually.)

To research a topic in C.F.R., you may use the general index published with the set or *West's Code of Federal Regulations: General Index*. Look up your research terms or the relevant agency's name, and then read the regulations referenced. It may be more efficient to begin your research in an annotated statutory code that contains references to related regulations for each statute. After finding a statute on point, review the annotations following the statutory language for cross-references to relevant regulations; you may notice that *United States Code Service* (U.S.C.S.) tends to provide more references to regulations than does *United States Code Annotated* (U.S.C.A.) Look up the citations given and review the regulations.

Another print product available for selected areas of law is *West's Code of Federal Regulations Annotated* for title 8 (Aliens & Nationality), title 29 (Labor), title 42 (Medicare/Medicaid), and title 49 (Transportation). These sets provide the full text of regulations along with related case summaries, law review and journal commentary references, and references to corollary provisions of U.S.C.A. The online counterpart, *Regulations Plus*, is available on Westlaw.

**Table 6-7. Examples of Federal Regulations
(28 C.F.R. 551.4 and 28 C.F.R. 551.5)**

```
TITLE 28—JUDICIAL ADMINISTRATION
CHAPTER V—BUREAU OF PRISONS, DEPARTMENT OF JUSTICE
PART 551 MISCELLANEOUS—Table of Contents
Subpart A Grooming

Sec. 551.4 Hair length.

 (a) The Warden may not restrict hair length if
the inmate keeps it neat and clean.
 (b) The Warden shall require an inmate with long
hair to wear a cap or hair net when working in
food service or where long hair could result in
increased likelihood of work injury.
 (c) The Warden shall make available to an inmate
hair care services which comply with applicable
health and sanitation requirements.

[44 FR 38252, June 29, 1979, as amended at 46 FR
59509, Dec. 4, 1981]

Sec. 551.5 Restrictions and exceptions.

 The Warden may impose restrictions or exceptions
for documented medical reasons.
```

Source: *Code of Federal Regulations* via GPO Access. Revised as of July 1, 2006, available at www.gpoaccess.gov/cfr/index.html.

Federal regulations are available online via GPO Access from 1996 to the present at www.gpoaccess.gov/cfr/index.html. The website allows searching by keyword, citation, and title. Table 6-7 provides an example of federal regulations from the GPO Access website. The C.F.R. is also available on LexisNexis and Westlaw.

B. *Federal Register*

New regulations and proposed changes to existing regulations are published first in the *Federal Register*, the federal equivalent of *Geor-*

gia Government Register. The *Federal Register* is the official daily publication for rules, proposed rules, and notices of federal agencies and organizations, as well as executive orders and other presidential documents. It is published almost every weekday, with continuous pagination throughout the year. This means that page numbers in the thousands are common. The online version of the *Federal Register* is available at www.gpoaccess.gov/fr/index.html, in addition to Lexis-Nexis, Loislaw, and Westlaw.

C. Updating Federal Regulations

Updating regulations refers to the process of determining if the text of a regulation has changed or if the regulation has been repealed. To update a federal regulation in print or on the government's website, begin with a small booklet or the database called *List of CFR Sections Affected* (LSA). As its name suggests, LSA lists all sections of C.F.R. that have been affected by recent agency action. The LSA provides page references to *Federal Register* issues where action affecting a section of C.F.R. is included. If the section you are researching is not listed in LSA, then it has not been changed since its annual revision. LSA is issued monthly; however, on GPO Access at http://www.gpoaccess.gov/lsa/index.html, the LSA also contains three supplemental services: *Last Month's List of CFR Sections Affected, Current List of CFR Parts Affected*, and the *List of CFR Parts Affected Today*. A complete list of steps for updating federal regulations using the print and online LSA are provided in Tables 6-8 and 6-9.

In addition to updating federal regulations with the LSA, you can also update them by using Shepard's or KeyCite. Note that when you retrieve a regulation online using fee-based databases you are viewing the most current form of the regulation unless otherwise noted. Therefore, the value of using Shepard's or KeyCite for federal regulations is in the treatment codes and other editorial analysis.

D. Researching Agency Decisions

Like Georgia agencies, federal agencies hold quasi-judicial hearings to decide cases that arise under the agencies' regulations. Some

Table 6-8. Updating Federal Regulations Using the Print LSA

Step One	Note the date of the C.F.R. volume containing the section you want to update.
Step Two	Locate the most current LSA that updates your C.F.R. title. The tables inside list the C.F.R. sections that have been amended or repealed, and, if a section is affected, a page number where the text of this change appears in the *Federal Register* will be provided. At this point, you have updated your C.F.R. section through the time period noted on the cover of the LSA pamphlet used.
Step Three	To complete final updating, refer to a table at the back of the *Federal Register* called "CFR Parts Affected During [the current month]." Do not confuse this table with the "CFR Parts Affected in this [Current] Issue" located in the Contents at the beginning of each issue. Refer to this table in each *Federal Register* for the last day of each month for all the months between the most recent monthly LSA issue and the current date. Also check the most recent issue of *Federal Register* for the present month. The table contains more general information—whether a "part" has been affected, not a "section"—but will note changes made since the most recent LSA.

of these decisions are published in reporters specific to each agency, for example, *Decisions and Orders of the National Labor Relations Board* (N.L.R.B.) A list of selected agency reporters is available in an online "appendix" to the *ALWD Manual* at www.alwd.org/cm. A list of selected agency reporters is also available in T.1 of the *Bluebook*.

E. Researching Judicial Opinions

The method of case research explained in Chapter 3 will lead to opinions in which the judiciary reviewed decisions of federal agencies. Additionally, *Shepard's Code of Federal Regulations Citations* in print and online, and its Westlaw counterpart KeyCite, are useful research tools both for updating federal regulations and for finding cases relevant to regulatory research. The process of updating is described in Chapter 7.

Table 6-9. Updating Federal Regulations Online via GPO Access

Step One	Consult the *List of CFR Sections Affected* located at www.gpoaccess.gov/lsa/index.html to locate changes in C.F.R. sections this month. If your section is affected, a *Federal Register* page number will be provided so that you can locate the text of the change.
	If your section is not affected, it will not be listed.
Step Two	Consult the table "Last Month's List of CFR Parts Affected" located at www.gpoaccess.gov/lsa/index.html to locate changes in C.F.R. parts last month. If your part is affected, a *Federal Register* page number will be provided so that you can locate the text of the change.
	If your part is not affected, it will not be listed.
Step Three	Consult the table "Current List of CFR Parts Affected" located at www.gpoaccess.gov/lsa/index.html to locate C.F.R. parts affected by changes since the last monthly issue of the LSA. If your part is affected, a *Federal Register* page number will be provided so that you can locate the text of the change.
	If your part is not affected, it will not be listed.
Step Four	Consult the "List of CFR Parts Affected Today" located at www.gpoaccess.gov/lsa/index.html to locate C.F.R. parts affected by changes appearing in most current issue *Federal Register*. If your part is affected, a *Federal Register* page number will be provided so that you can locate the text of the change.
	If your part is not affected, it will not be listed.

Appendix 6-A. Online Sources of Georgia Agency Rules

CASEMAKER—free to members of the State Bar of Georgia www.gabar.org/casemaker	
Content	Rules and regulations of the State of Georgia
Coverage	Current
Update	Updated twenty-one days from release
Notes	Search by keyword or browse by chapter
GEORGIA SECRETARY OF STATE—free www.sos.state.ga.us/rules_regs.htm	
Content	Rules and regulations of the State of Georgia
Coverage	Current
Update	Monthly
Notes	Search by keyword or browse by agency
GEORGIA.GOV: ONLINE ACCESS TO GEORGIA GOVERNMENT—free www.georgia.gov	
Content	Provides links to Georgia agency websites
Coverage	Some rules are linked from agency websites
LEXISNEXIS—commercial www.lexis.com	
Content	Georgia Government Register
Coverage	Georgia Government Register (January 2002 to present)
Update	As received from publisher
Notes	Tracks rulemaking activity in Georgia; not a full-text source of rules but is a full-text source of changes to rules
LEXISNEXIS—commercial www.lexis.com	
Content	Rules and regulations of the State of Georgia
Coverage	Current rules available
Update	Updated when received from the Secretary of State
Notes	Administrative Archive containing the text of the Georgia Administrative Code for each year beginning in 2004. Georgia Administrative Regulations Tracking database includes summaries of proposed rules and status actions for individual rules promulgated by various agencies in the state.

Appendix 6-A. Online Sources of Georgia Agency Rules, cont'd

LOISLAW — commercial www.loislaw.com	
Content	Rules and regulations of the State of Georgia
Coverage	Current rules available
Update	Updated when received from the Secretary of State

WESTLAW — commercial www.westlaw.com	
Content	Rules and regulations of the State of Georgia
Coverage	Current rules available
Update	Updated when received from the Secretary of State

Appendix 6-B. Online Sources of Agency Decisions

LEXISNEXIS — commercial www.lexis.com	
Content	Full text
Coverage	Georgia Commissioner of Securities Decisions (February 1973 to September 1998)
	Georgia Department of Natural Resources Decisions (April 1973 to present)
	Georgia Public Service Commission Decisions (November 2, 1999 to present)
	Georgia Judicial Qualifications Commission Opinions (1997–present)
Update	Updated as received from the agency

STATE BOARD OF EDUCATION —free www.doe.k12.ga.us (click on "Appeals and Decisions")	
Content	Appeals decisions only
Coverage	1975–present
Update	Current
Notes	Search by keyword or browse by year

WESTLAW — commercial www.westlaw.com	
Content	Full text
Coverage	Georgia Attorney General Opinions (1977–present)
	Georgia Environmental Law Administrative Decisions (1975–present)
	Georgia Public Utilities Reports (1953–present)
Update	Updated when received from the agency

Appendix 6-C. Online Sources of Attorney General Opinions

CASEMAKER—free to members of the State Bar of Georgia http://www.gabar.org/casemaker	
Content	Attorney General Opinions
Coverage	1994–present
Update	Updated ten days from release
LEXISNEXIS—commercial www.lexis.com	
Content	Attorney General Opinions
Coverage	1970–present
Update	Updated when received from the State
OFFICE OF THE ATTORNEY GENERAL OF GEORGIA—free www.ganet.org/ago/opinions.html	
Content	Attorney General Opinions
Coverage	1994–present
Update	Current
Notes	Search by keyword or number; contact the Office of the Attorney General for copies of Attorney General Opinions prior to 1994
WESTLAW—commercial www.westlaw.com	
Content	Attorney General Opinions
Coverage	1977–present
Update	Updated when received from the State

Appendix 6-D. Online Sources of Governor Executive Orders and Proclamations

GEORGIA GOVERNOR'S WEBSITE—free	
www.gov.state.ga.us	
Content	Executive Orders (at http://www.gov.state.ga.us/2005_exec_orders.shtml)
	Proclamations (at http://www.gov.state.ga.us/proclamations.shtml)
Coverage	Current administration only
Update	As issued by the Governor
Notes	Governor Executive Orders and Proclamations from previous administrations can be accessed at the Georgia Archives located in Morrow, Georgia (or call (678) 364-3700 for assistance)
LEXISNEXIS—commercial	
www.lexis.com	
Content	Georgia Government Register
Coverage	January 2002 to present
Update	As received from the publisher

Chapter 7

Updating Research with Citators

After reading this chapter you will:

- understand the importance of updating legal authorities you are relying on;
- know when to update legal authorities you are relying on;
- understand the fundamental aspects of using an online citator;
- recognize the differences between various online citator services; and
- know the fundamentals of updating with print sources and understand what is unique about the print *Shepard's Georgia Citations.*

I. Why Update with Citators?

Before using any legal authority to analyze a problem, you must know how that authority has been treated by later actions of a court, legislature, or agency. A case may have been reversed or overruled; a statute or regulation may have been amended or repealed. Pocket parts in digests and annotated codes provide access to newer law, but they do not indicate the status of older authority you may have located. Ensuring that the cases, statutes, and other authorities you rely on represent the *current* law requires an additional step; the generic term for this step is "updating," though it is often called "Shepardizing" because the first major updating tool was *Shepard's Citations.*

To update an authority, you must find every subsequent legal source that has cited your authority and determine how the subsequent source treated your authority on a particular issue. To begin, you need a list of citations to sources that refer to your authority. A *citator* provides that list.

This chapter focuses on updating cases with online sources. This chapter focuses on updating cases because cases are the authorities most often updated. Other authorities—including statutes, constitutional provisions, regulations, and some secondary sources—can be updated and will be addressed briefly. This chapter concentrates on updating with online sources because they are more current than print citators. Print citators tend to lag behind their online counterparts by at least a few months, posing a risk to the validity of your research. Whether you choose a print or online citator, you must take the time to interpret the information presented and read the later authorities to determine how they affect your analysis.

II. When to Update

Updating can be a valuable research tool at several points in the research process. Some researchers update cases as soon as they find them. A researcher following this method knows immediately whether a case is still respected authority. At the same time, the researcher also finds other cases and secondary sources that discuss the same points of law as the first case.

Other researchers update cases later in the research process. In this instance, the researcher would begin by finding cases in annotated statutes and in digests, read the cases, begin to outline an argument, and then update only the cases that will likely appear in the memorandum. This researcher will have to update fewer cases, but may have started to develop a line of analysis that is no longer "good law." In this case, the researcher may need to do additional research or may need to rethink the argument. Moreover, this researcher will not be using a citator as a research tool for finding additional cases and secondary sources.

Regardless of when you decide to update, whether early or late in the research process, the end result should be that you find all current and relevant authorities for your legal issues. You should continue updating cases and other authorities until the moment your final document is submitted, and again prior to any hearings, trials, or other actions associated with your case. Simply stated, failure to update thoroughly is a disservice to your client and is grounds for malpractice.

III. Online Citators

Online citators include Shepard's (LexisNexis), KeyCite (Westlaw), GlobalCite (Loislaw), and CaseCheck (Casemaker). Use of online citators is recommended over print citators because they are easier to use and provide the most comprehensive, up-to-date information about the status of an authority.

Researchers generally consider Shepard's and KeyCite to be the most comprehensive online case citators available. Shepard's has been available as a resource in the legal community for over 100 years, and KeyCite has been an online product in the legal marketplace since 1997. GlobalCite and CaseCheck are newcomers in the online citator arena and provide little or no analysis compared to their elder competitors.

Researchers without access to an online citator have a few options. They can seek institutions in the community such as public and academic libraries that may subscribe to and provide public access to these online citator services. A researcher may also purchase a subscription or subscribe by credit card on the LexisNexis or Westlaw websites to Shepard's or KeyCite for a single use or an a la carte service.

IV. Online Case Citators

When you update a case, your main goal is to determine whether the case has been overruled or reversed. If it has been overruled or reversed, you must determine whether it was overruled or reversed for the same issue or point of law that you are relying on. For example, if you are relying on a case for its support of a substantive issue and the case was reversed because of a procedural issue (or even a different substantive issue), you can still rely on this case with an explanation of this distinction. If the case has not been overruled or reversed, you must explore the subsequent treatment of this case by other courts to assess the impact on its precedential value. Shepard's and KeyCite provide different tools to make this assessment.

A. Updating with Shepard's and KeyCite

Both Shepard's and KeyCite produce comprehensive reports with information about the case you are updating. Both include colored symbols that quickly tell you that service's opinion about the value of the case you are updating. Both services use a similar spectrum of color codes ranging from red (connoting negative treatment by later cases) to blue (connoting positive or neutral treatment by later cases). Table 7-1 includes information about each *Shepard's* Signal™ and KeyCite symbol.

1. Updating Basics

Although novice researchers are tempted to rely strictly on the colored symbols provided by Shepard's and KeyCite, doing so can be perilous. You know your research project better than an anonymous attorney-editor employed by one of the services to make generic determinations about the value of cases. Thus, you need to read the citing references and form your own judgment about whether a particular authority is valuable for your analysis.

Both Shepard's (shown in Table 7-2) and KeyCite (shown in Tables 7-3 and 7-4) produce comprehensive lists of other authorities that cite your case; these authorities are referred to as *citing references*. These references include later cases, secondary sources, and other material available on that service that cite your case.

In addition to providing lists of citing references, Shepard's and KeyCite both indicate how the citing references treated your case. Shepard's uses descriptive phrases such as "distinguished by," "cited

Table 7-1. Case Treatment Symbols

Treatment Category	KeyCite	Shepard's
Negative Treatment	Red Flag *No longer good for at least one point of law*	Red Stop Sign *Warning: Negative treatment is indicated*
Possible Negative Treatment	Yellow Flag *Some negative history but not overruled*	Orange Q *Questioned: Validity questioned by citing references* Yellow Triangle *Caution: Possible negative treatment*
Positive or Neutral Treatment	Green C *Citing references available* Blue H *Case has some history*	Green Plus Sign *Positive treatment indicated* Blue A *Citing references with analysis available* Blue I *Citation information available*

by," or "mentioned" to express how a case has been treated. KeyCite uses depth of treatment stars: one or two stars means your case was merely mentioned or cited; three stars means the case was discussed; and four stars means the case was examined at some length.

Both Shepard's and KeyCite offer two levels of updating—one simply to determine whether the case has been reversed or overruled and another to find an exhaustive list of all citing references. The more limited list provides the "history" of the case you are updating. The more expansive list is useful when using one case as a launching point in research to find additional cases.

On Shepard's, clicking the radio button "Shepard's for Validation" produces a list of citing sources limited to Georgia decisions, a Shepard's summary limited to Georgia decisions and headnotes, and the subsequent appellate history. By contrast, clicking the radio button "Shepard's for Research" produces a list of all sources in the LexisNexis system that have cited your case. An example of Shepard's for Research is shown in Table 7-2. On KeyCite, the default setting is usually "Full History." While that name implies a full listing of citing references, Full History gives just the history of the case you are updating. Thus, Full History is similar to Shepard's for Validation. To find a complete list of citing references on KeyCite, click on the link "Citing References" in the left frame.

Although both services contain a lot of similar information, they are organized differently and do not contain the same features. Shepard's provides a summary of the Shepard's report first. This summary information is designed to give a first impression about the status of a case. It includes a Shepard's symbol showing the status of the case you are updating and hyperlinks to citing cases by categories such as "Concurring Opinion" or "Dissenting Opinion." Next, Shepard's lists the history of the case you are updating; this is the litigation trail of your case, showing the results of various appeals. Third, Shepard's provides citing references. Cases are arranged by jurisdiction, followed by secondary sources.

KeyCite begins with the "Direct History," which is the procedural history of the case. Direct History is available in text form (Table 7-3) or in chart form known as "Graphical KeyCite." After reviewing the Direct History, click on the "Citing References" link in the left frame. "Negative Cases" and "Positive Cases" are listed respectively. In addition to the depth of treatment stars, KeyCite provides purple quotation marks to convey that the citing reference includes a quote in its discussion of the case you are updating. A visual example of depth of treatment stars and purple quotation marks is in Table 7-4.

2. Comparison of KeyCite and Shepard's

With this understanding of the technical differences between these services, we are ready to explore the differences in the process of updating a case with KeyCite and Shepard's using the Georgia case *Christensen v. State*. Each step of the process is emphasized in **bold** font in Table 7-5.

Table 7-2. Shepard's for Research on LexisNexis

LexisNexis® *Total Research System*

Custom ID ▼ No Description | Sub

Search | Research Tasks | Search Advisor | Get a Document | Shepard's® | Alerts

Shepardize® [Go ►]

View: KWIC | Full
Display Options ►

◄ 1 - 50 of 51 Total Cites [NEXT]

Save As *Shepard's* Alert® | Unrestricted | All Neg | All Pos | FOCUS™ Restrict By

Shepard's® Ⓐ Christensen v. State, 266 Ga. 474 (TOA)

Unrestricted *Shepard's* Summary

Ⓞ No negative subsequent appellate history.

Citing References:

Ⓞ Neutral Analyses: Concurring Opinion (4), Dissenting Op. (2)

Other Sources: Law Reviews (39), Statutes (2), Treatises (1)

LexisNexis Headnotes: HN1 (1), HN2 (2)

Show full text of headnotes

PRIOR HISTORY (0 citing references) ♦ Hide Prior History

► (CITATION YOU ENTERED):
Christensen v. State, 266 Ga. 474, 468 S.E.2d 188, 1996 Ga. LEXIS 115, 96 Fulton County D. Rep. P884 (1996)

SUBSEQUENT APPELLATE HISTORY (1 citing reference) ♦ Hide Subsequent Appellate History

✔ Select for Delivery

☐ 1. **Reconsideration denied by, (Mar. 28, 1996)**

CITING DECISIONS (8 citing decisions)

GEORGIA SUPREME COURT

☐ 2. **Cited in Dissenting Opinion at, Cited by:**
Powell v. State, 270 Ga. 327, 510 S.E.2d 18, 1998 Ga. LEXIS 1148, 98 Fulton County D. Rep. 4177 (1998) LexisNexis Headnotes HN2

Cited in Dissenting Opinion at:
270 Ga. 327 p.338
510 S E 2d 18 p 29

Table 7-3. KeyCite Direct History

KeyCite

△

⊕ QUICK PRINT   ⊕ PRINT   ✉ EMAIL   ⊕ DOWNLOAD   ☒ OTHER

Christensen v. State
266 Ga. 474, 468 S.E.2d 188
Ga.,1996.
March 11, 1996

FOR EDUCATIONAL USE ONLY

History
(Showing 7 documents)

Direct History

↳ SELECT TO PRINT, EMAIL, ETC.

☐ ↑ 1 KeyCited Citation:
Christensen v. State, 266 Ga. 474, 468 S.E.2d 188 (Ga. Mar 11, 1996) (NO. S95A1586), reconsideration denied (Mar 28, 1996)

Called into Doubt by

☐ ▷ 2 Powell v. State, 270 Ga. 327, 510 S.E.2d 18, 98 FCDR 3952 (Ga. Nov 23, 1998) (NO. S98A0755), reconsideration denied (Dec 17, 1998) ★ ★ ★ ★ **HN: 2,3,4 (S.E.2d)**

Negative Citing References (U.S.A.)

Reprinted from Westlaw with permission of Thomson/West.

Table 7-4. KeyCite Citing References

Christensen v. State
266 Ga. 474, 468 S.E.2d 188
Ga., 1996.
March 11, 1996

FOR EDUCATIONAL USE ONLY

Citing References
(Showing 72 documents)

Negative Cases (U.S.A.)

SELECT TO PRINT, EMAIL, ETC.

Called into Doubt by

☆☆☆☆ HN: 2,3,4 (S.E.2d)

□ ▷ 1 Powell v. State, 510 S.E.2d 18, 24+, 270 Ga. 327, 333+, 98 FCDR 3952, 3952+ (Ga. Nov 23, 1998) (NO. S98A0755) 99

Positive Cases (U.S.A.)
☆☆ Cited

□ ▷ 2 Phagan v. State, 486 S.E.2d 876, 879+, 268 Ga. 272, 274+, 97 FCDR 2622, 2622+ (Ga. Jul 16, 1997) (NO. S97A0161)
99 HN: 2,3 (S.E.2d)

H 3 Shahar v. Bowers, 114 F.3d 1097, 1105, 65 USLW 2795, 2795, 70 Empl. Prac. Dec. P 44,739, 44739, 12 IER Cases 1582, 1582, 11 Fla. L. Weekly Fed. C 36, 36 (11th Cir.(Ga.) May 30, 1997) (NO. 93-9345)

□ ▷ 4 Jegley v. Picado, 80 S.W.3d 332, 355, 349 Ark. 600, 640 (Ark. Jul 05, 2002) (NO. 01-815)

□ ▷ 5 State v. Smith, 766 So.2d 501, 510+, 99-2015 (La. 7/6/00), 7/6/00+, 99-2019 (La. 7/6/00+, 99-2094 (La. 7/6/00)+, 1999-0606 (La. 7/6/00)+ (La. Jul 06, 2000) (NO. 99-KA-0606, 99-KA-2094, 99-KA-2015, 99-KA-2019) HN: 3 (S.E.2d)

□ ● 6 Williams v. Glendening, 1998 WL 965992, *7 (Md.Cir.Ct. Oct 15, 1998) (NO. 98036031/CL-1059) HN: 3 (S.E.2d)

★ Mentioned

□ ● 7 Matter of Holloway, 469 S.E.2d 167, 170, 266 Ga. 599, 603 (Ga. Apr 29, 1996) (NO. S95Y0195`)

Reprinted from Westlaw with permission of Thomson/West.

Table 7-5 (next page). Steps for Updating with KeyCite and Shepard's Online Using *Christensen v. State*, 266 Ga. 474, 468 S.E.2d 188 (1996)

Step	KeyCite	Shepard's
1	**Login** at www.westlaw.com.	**Login** at www.lexis.com.
2	Click on the "KeyCite" link at the top of the page or use the "KeyCite this citation" box in the left frame of the page.	Click on the tan-colored "Shepard's" tab at the top of the page.
3	Enter the full citation: 266 Ga. 474	Enter the full citation: 266 Ga. 474
4	Look for the KeyCite symbol to begin your assessment of this case. There is a yellow flag, which means *Some Negative History But Not Overruled.*	Look for the Shepard's symbol to begin your assessment of this case. There is a blue circle with an A inside, which means *Citing References with Analysis Available.*
5	How has this case been treated by Georgia courts? Explore why there is possible negative treatment of *Christensen* by evaluating the *citing references* in Georgia first. Click on the "Citing References" link in the left frame of the page. To limit the number of citing references, click on the "Limit KeyCite Display" button at the bottom of the page to limit the citing references by jurisdiction, document type, date, depth of treatment, or headnote. To evaluate the relevance of citing opinions use the depth of treatment codes and other editorial analysis. You can also click on the hyperlink number next to the citing decision. This will open the full text of the citing opinion and take you to the area that mentions *Christensen*. Evaluating this area of the citing opinion should help you decide whether the citing opinion has any impact on the standing of your case for your legal issue.	How has this case been treated by Georgia courts? Explore the treatment of *Christensen* by evaluating the *citing decisions* in Georgia first. Scroll down to the section marked *Citing Decisions*. To limit the number of citing references, use the *Focus™-Restrict By* link to limit your citing references by date, jurisdiction, Lexis headnote number, type of analysis, or *Focus* keyword. To evaluate the relevance of citing opinions, click on the hyperlink in the pinpoint cite below the citing case. This will open the full text of the citing opinion and take you to the area that mentions *Christensen*. Evaluating this area of the citing opinion should help you decide whether the citing opinion has any impact on the standing of your case for your legal issue.
6	After evaluating the Georgia cases, **evaluate the citing references in the Eleventh Circuit or other federal courts.**	After evaluating the Georgia cases, **evaluate the citing references in the Eleventh Circuit or other federal courts.**
7	Use related documents and secondary sources. Evaluate whether the related documents listed at the end of the KeyCite report add anything to your research generally or to your assessment of whether *Christensen* is still good law. Related documents include statutes, law review articles, encyclopedias, treatises, and other related resources available on Westlaw.	Use related documents and secondary sources. Evaluate whether the related documents listed at the end of the Shepard's report add anything to your research generally or to your assessment of whether *Christensen* is still good law. Related documents include statutes, law review articles, encyclopedias, treatises, and other related resources available on LexisNexis.

There are philosophical differences between these two citator services as exemplified by the different treatment codes assigned to *Christensen*. This case was called into doubt by the KeyCite attorney-editors and assigned a yellow flag to indicate some negative history. After an exploration of why *Christensen* was called into doubt, you will see that the yellow flag was assigned because *Christensen* was cast in a negative light in the dissent of a subsequent case. On the other hand, the Shepard's attorney-editors assigned a neutral symbol to *Christensen* and noted the dissent by stating "Cited in Dissenting Opinion" with the citing reference. Both approaches are acceptable. However, an astute researcher must be aware of these different approaches and factor them into the use of these services. Most of all, the astute researcher must read the citing references and analyze them independently of the services' symbols.

3. Graphical KeyCite

Many cases have a complex history. You can view the history of a case in a color-coded diagram format in Westlaw's Graphical KeyCite service. Indirect history and citing references are not available in Graphical KeyCite. You will have to use the traditional KeyCite service for this information.

4. KeyCite Alert and Shepard's Alert

You can monitor the status of cases by using alert services available in KeyCite and Shepard's. To set up KeyCite Alert from within a KeyCite report, click on the "Monitor With KeyCite Alert" link. The setup wizard will guide you through the rest of the process. To monitor the status of a case in Shepard's, click on the "Save As Shepard's Alert" link at the top of the page. The next screen will allow you to customize your Shepard's Alert.

5. Using Online Citators to Find Cases

Citators are excellent case-finding tools. If you have one relevant case, use a citator to find other relevant cases from the history of the case or from the citing references list. In Shepard's and KeyCite, you have the ability to restrict or limit your citing references by jurisdiction, headnote number, or case treatment.

One case-finding feature of KeyCite and Shepard's is the Table of Authorities. This feature allows you to compile a list of cases cited by a case. The list includes treatment codes so that you are able to easily select the cases worth pursuing. Images of the Table of Authorities for KeyCite and Shepard's are available in Tables 7-6 and 7-7, respectively.

B. Updating with CaseCheck and GlobalCite

Casemaker's citator service, CaseCheck, is available at no charge to members of the State Bar of Georgia. When you retrieve a case, CaseCheck automatically supplies citing references from cases available in the Casemaker database. However, aside from supplying citing cases, CaseCheck provides no treatment codes, editorial analysis, or other related authorities.

GlobalCite is accessible through Loislaw. You must retrieve the full text of a case and choose the GlobalCite option at the bottom of the screen. GlobalCite retrieves a list of citing cases or other materials available in the Loislaw databases that cite the case. Like CaseCheck, GlobalCite provides no treatment codes or other authorities aside from citing cases.

V. Online Statutory Citators

Once you find relevant statutory language, you should search for judicial decisions that have interpreted the statute or have clarified ambiguous statutory language. Once a court interprets a statute, the interpretation itself becomes an integral part of understanding the statute.[1] As discussed in Chapters 2 and 4, one of the easiest places to locate decisions that have interpreted statutes is in the annotations of the *Official Code of Georgia Annotated* or *West's Code of Georgia Annotated*.

---

1. *See Jones v. Swett*, 244 Ga. 715, 717 (1979).

Table 7-6. Table of Authorities for *Christensen v. State* in KeyCite

KeyCite
△

Christensen v. State
266 Ga. 474, 468 S.E.2d 188
Ga., 1996.
March 11, 1996

36 Cases Cited in Christensen v. State

C 1 Anderson v. State, 235 S.E.2d 675 (Ga.App. 1977)
★★
189

△ 2 Barnes v. Glen Theatre, Inc., 111 S.Ct. 2456 (U.S.Ind. 1991)
★★
190

△ 3 Blincoe v. State, 204 S.E.2d 597 (Ga. 1974) 99
★★★
190+

▲ 4 Bowers v. Hardwick, 106 S.Ct. 2841 (U.S.Ga. 1986) 99
★★★★
190+

△ 5 Brandenburg v. Ohio, 89 S.Ct. 1827 (U.S.Ohio 1969) 99
★★★★
190+

△ 6 Broadrick v. Oklahoma, 93 S.Ct. 2908 (U.S.Okla. 1973) 99
★★★★
189+

△ 7 Campbell v. Sundquist, 926 S.W.2d 250 (Tenn.Ct.App. 1996) *(dissent)*
★★
192+

Reprinted from Westlaw with permission of Thomson/West.

Table 7-7. Table of Authorities for *Christensen v. State* in Shepard's

LexisNexis® *Total Research System*
Search | Research Tasks | Search Advisor | Get a Document | Shepard's® | Alerts

New TOA: [   ] [Go →]

View: **Full**
Show Parallel Cites

Signal: ⓐ Citing Refs. With Analysis Available (Legend)
Trail: **Unrestricted**

◀◀◀ **1 - 40 of 40 Total Cites** ▶▶▶
Return to *Shepard's*   Unrestricted | FOCUS™. Restrict By
Shepard's® **TABLE OF AUTHORITIES for:** 266 Ga. 474

Christensen v. State, 266 Ga. 474, 468 S.E.2d 188, 1996 Ga. LEXIS 115, 96 Fulton County D. Rep. P884 (1996)

TABLE OF AUTHORITIES (Copyright 2007 SHEPARD'S Company. All rights reserved.)

40 DECISION(S) CITED BY: 266 Ga. 474

✔ Select for Delivery

☐ 1.   **Dissenting opinion citing:**
  U.S. Supreme Court
  Bowers v. Hardwick, 478 U.S. 186 (1986) ●
  First Ref: 266 Ga. 474 at p. 475

☐ 2.   **Following:**
  Jackson v. Virginia, 443 U.S. 307 (1979) ●
  First Ref: 266 Ga. 474 at p. 475

☐ 3.   **Citing:**
  Broadrick v. Oklahoma, 413 U.S. 601 (1973) 🅖
  First Ref: 266 Ga. 474 at p. 475

☐ 4.   **Citing:**
  Barnes v. Glen Theatre, Inc., 501 U.S. 560 (1991) ●
  First Ref: 266 Ga. 474 at p. 476

☐ 5.   **Dissenting opinion citing:**
  Brandenburg v. Ohio, 395 U.S. 444 (1969) ▲
  First Ref: 266 Ga. 474 at p. 476

Custom ID ▾ No Description | Switch Client | Preferences | Live Support
History ‖
FAST Print...   Print | Download | Fax | E

You can explore whether a statute has been repealed, amended, or has any citing references by using Shepard's, KeyCite, and GlobalCite. A unique feature of KeyCite is the availability of pending legislation that would affect the statute in question.

VI. Online Citators for Other Legal Materials

Online citators are available to update legal materials other than cases and statutes. For example, you can update federal regulations in KeyCite or Shepard's, but the only source for updating Georgia regulations is GlobalCite. In addition, you can run Georgia law review articles through KeyCite and Shepard's for citing references. Table 7-8 compares the four online citators discussed in this chapter.

Table 7-8. Comparison of Online Citators

	CaseCheck www.gabar.org/ casemaker	GlobalCite www.loislaw.com	KeyCite www.westlaw.com	Shepard's www.lexis.com
Free or Commercial	Free to members of the State Bar of Georgia	Commercial	Commercial	Commercial
Print or Online	Online	Online	Online	Both
Case Citator	Included	Included	Included	Included
Georgia Reports (Ga.)	1939–present	1939–present	1846–present	1846–present
Georgia Appeals Reports (Ga. App.)	1939–present	1939–present	1907–present	1907–present
Statutory Citator	Not included	Included	Included	Included
Regulations Citator	Federal only	State and federal	Federal only	Federal only
Law Review Article Citator	Not included	Not included	Included	Included
References to Secondary Sources Owned by Vendor	Not included	Included	Included	Included

Table 7-9. Citator Tutorials Available Online

GlobalCite	www.llrx.com/features/globalsite.htm
KeyCite	http://west.thomson.com/KeyCite/KeyCite.pdf
Shepard's (online)	http://web.lexis.com/help/multimedia/ shepards.htm
Shepard's (print)	www.lexisnexis.com/shepards/printsupport/ shepardize_print.pdf

VII. Online Tutorials

If your updating needs are beyond the scope of this chapter, consult Table 7-9 to locate vendor-sponsored tutorials available online.

VIII. Print Citators

When updating Georgia law in print, the available citators include *Shepard's Georgia Citations* and *Shepard's South Eastern Citations.* Each of these citators uses a combination of bound volumes and supplementary pamphlets to list the citing references that are summarized in one place on an online citator.

To know which volumes and pamphlets you need to update a particular authority, refer to the most recent pamphlet. Usually this will be a red-cover pamphlet that is no more than one month old. On the cover you will see a box entitled "What Your Library Should Contain." Gather the volumes and pamphlets listed there, and look up your authority in each.

Listed under your authority will be its citing references. Note that each volume or pamphlet contains citing references from a specific period; they are not cumulative, so you must check each one for a complete list of citing references. Introductory pages at the front of each volume or supplement show how to interpret the citing references and the symbols that show how they treated your authority.

There is a considerable time lag from when new information becomes available and when it is printed in *Shepard's* and subsequently made available on library shelves. Relying on a citator that is not timely can pose both practical and ethical concerns.[2] Caution must be exercised about complete reliance on a print citator for updating.

Despite the undesirable aspects of print citators, the ability to Shepardize code sections from the 1933 Code of Georgia, titled *Code of Georgia of 1933 — Georgia Code Annotated*, is unique to the print *Shepard's Georgia Citations*.

The citing references in *Shepard's Georgia Citations* and *Shepard's South Eastern Citations* are not identical. Table 7-10 provides a comparison of the two print citators that update Georgia cases.

Table 7-10. Comparison of Citing References in Print Citators (for Georgia Cases)

Citing References	*Shepard's Georgia Citations*	*Shepard's South Eastern Citations*
Georgia Laws	Included	Not included
Georgia Cases	Included	Included
Out-of-State Cases	Not included	Included (North Carolina, South Carolina, Virginia, and West Virginia)
Federal Cases	Included	Included
A.L.R. Annotations	Included	Included
Legal Treatises	Included	Not included
Law Review Articles	Selected law review articles from any jurisdiction included	Not included

---

2. *See* Ga. Ethics Rule 1.1, *Competence*, available at www.gabar.org/handbook/part_iv_after_january_1_2001_-_georgia_rules_of_professional_conduct/rule_11_competence.

Chapter 8

Secondary Sources and Practice Materials

After reading this chapter you will be able to:

- recognize the value of secondary sources for legal research;
- identify the different sources of secondary material; and
- know how and when to use these sources during the research process.

I. Secondary Sources

Other lawyers have previously researched and analyzed many of the issues that you will face in law practice. Many have published their work in legal encyclopedias, treatises, law review articles, practice handbooks, and other secondary sources. These sources are "secondary" because they are written by law professors, practicing attorneys, legal editors, and even law students. In contrast, "primary" authority is written by legislatures, courts, and administrative agencies.

Lawyers use secondary sources to learn about the law and to find references to relevant primary authority. Often, beginning a new research project in a secondary source will be more effective than beginning immediately to search for statutes or cases on point. By locating and understanding secondary sources on point, you can more easily comprehend the analysis of your problem and more quickly find pertinent primary authority. The text of a secondary source will likely explain terminology and concepts unfamiliar to you. This will make it possible for you to develop a more effective list of research

Table 8-1. Outline for Researching Secondary Sources

1. Generate a list of research terms.

2. Search your library's catalog or an online directory for relevant sources.

3. Search the index of a secondary source, browse the table of contents, or run a search online.

4. Find the relevant portion in the main volumes or link to the relevant online portion. Reading the commentary will assist your comprehension of the legal issues. Within the commentary, often in footnotes, you will find references to primary authority.

5. In print, check pocket parts or supplements to find more recent material in the secondary sources if possible.

terms. It will also help you understand the cases and statutes when you read them. Secondary sources often provide a shortcut to researching primary authority by including numerous references to cases, statutes, and rules.

This chapter introduces the most commonly used secondary sources including practice materials, continuing legal education (CLE) publications, legal encyclopedias, legal periodicals (including law reviews and bar journals), *American Law Reports* (a commentary-reporter), treatises and other books, topical "mini-libraries," forms, restatements, and jury instructions. The process for researching secondary sources varies depending on the source. A general outline is provided in Table 8-1.

II. Practice Materials

Practice materials are written on specific areas of law. These materials are written for attorneys to use in everyday practice as they encounter real situations. This means that the materials both explain the current state of the law and include citations to primary sources, forms, and practice tips. West and LexisNexis are the primary publishers of practice guides for Georgia. Most of the titles published by LexisNexis are available online and likewise the West titles are available on Westlaw.

Practice materials exist on a wide variety of subjects, including wills, criminal law, civil procedure, torts, and workers' compensation. Georgia real estate attorneys rely on *Pindar's Georgia Real Estate Law & Procedure* to find relevant law. If you find yourself in a family law practice, you will use McConaughey's *Georgia Divorce, Alimony and Child Custody*. You can turn to a practice treatise to get an overview of law if you are unfamiliar with the subject.

Many of the practice treatises are referred to by the original author's name. For example, the primary treatise on wills and administration of estates is referred to as Redfearn's though the current author is Mary F. Radford. The original author's name may or may not be in the title of the treatise; this fact may make it difficult to locate the book in a library catalog. You can use the selected list of Georgia practice materials in Appendix C of this book to familiarize yourself with the leading, most often used titles. The list is arranged by subject and includes only those treatises that have been updated within the last five years. The publishers update most of the books annually either with pocket parts or with new softbound editions.

A Georgia practice treatise on your topic is the best place to start your research. The book will outline and organize the law and cite to statutes, cases, and regulations. To use a practice treatise in print, search for your research terms in the index or scan the table of contents. Once you find the relevant sections that relate to your topic, be sure to read the sections before and after them to get an overview of your topic. Use the pocket part or supplementary pamphlet to update your research.

You can find additional practice material using the online catalogs of the Georgia law school libraries. Web addresses for the law libraries are included in Table 8-2.

Practice treatises are also available on Westlaw or LexisNexis in the respective "Georgia" directories. On Westlaw, the books are under the heading "Forms, Treatises, CLEs, and Other Practice Material," and,

Table 8-2. Websites of Law Schools and Law Libraries in Georgia

---

Emory University School of Law, Atlanta, Georgia
www.law.emory.edu
www.law.emory.edu/library (use search box under "Quick EU-
CLID Search")

Georgia State University College of Law, Atlanta, Georgia
http://law.gsu.edu
http://law.gsu.edu/library (click on "Library Catalog (GIL)")

John Marshall Law School, Atlanta, Georgia
www.johnmarshall.edu
www.johnmarshall.edu/library (click on "Online Library
Catalog")

Mercer University School of Law, Macon, Georgia
www.law.mercer.edu
www.law.mercer.edu/library (click on "Library Catalog-Law-
Cat")

University of Georgia School of Law, Athens, Georgia
www.law.uga.edu
www.law.uga.edu/library (click on "GAVEL-Catalog")

---

on LexisNexis, the treatises are under the heading "Treatises and Analytical Material."

You can either do a Terms and Connectors search or browse the book's table of contents online. Remember that you can "book browse," i.e., view neighboring sections of a book, online as well as in print. On Westlaw, use the links to "Previous Section" and "Next Section" that appear on the top of the screen beside the name of the book. On LexisNexis, first click the "Book Browse" button, then use the "Prev" and "Next" links at the top of the screen to browse the neighboring sections of the book.

One major resource for answering civil and criminal procedure questions is *Georgia Procedure* (*Ga. Proc.*) The coverage of this set is evident in the table of contents, reproduced in Table 8-3.

To use *Georgia Procedure*, look up your search terms in the Finding Aids volume, which will provide the relevant section numbers in

Table 8-3. Topics in *Georgia Procedure*

Civil Procedure
Court System and Types of Action
Considerations in Initiating Suit
Discovery, Pretrial Procedure and Conduct of Trial, Generally
Evidence
Verdict and Judgments
Post-Trial Motions and Appeals
Special Remedies and Proceedings
Criminal Procedure

Ga. Proc. You can use *Ga. Proc.* on Westlaw in the same way you would other practice treatises.

III. Continuing Legal Education Publications

Attorneys in Georgia are required to attend continuing legal education (CLE) courses periodically to maintain their membership in the state bar. These courses often present very practical information. Topics range from ethical issues in business law to building a personal injury practice. A CLE course may be aimed at new lawyers just learning the fundamentals of practice; however, many CLE courses are intended to offer new insights on cutting-edge legal issues. A CLE course may be led by a practitioner, judge, or law professor.

Frequently, the person leading the course prepares handouts that include sample forms, sample documents, and explanations. These handouts are compiled into books called program materials and are published without being typeset. The Institute of Continuing Legal Education in Georgia (ICLE) publishes many of these CLE program materials. Other publishers of similar materials are the Practising Law Institute (PLI), the American Law Institute (ALI), and the American Bar Association (ABA).

CLE materials are located by searching the library catalog by topic or by author, using the names of the more common CLE publishers as search terms. Always be sure that you use the most current material available by checking the library catalog and browsing the shelves nearby.

A list of publications for purchase is included on the website of the ICLE at www.iclega.org. To find publications that are not listed on the ICLE website or on any other website, search the online catalogs of Georgia law libraries (see web addresses in Table 8-2) and use "continuing legal education" in your search query.

You can also find a host of CLE materials on Westlaw and Lexis-Nexis. On Westlaw, you will find the PLI and National Business Institute materials as well as many state CLE materials in the "Forms, Treatises, CLEs, and Other Practice Material" area of the directory. On LexisNexis, the CLE materials in the "Secondary Legal > CLE Materials" library include the National Institute for Trial Advocacy and ALI-ABA materials.

IV. Legal Encyclopedias

Like other encyclopedias you may be familiar with, legal encyclopedias provide general information on a wide variety of legal subjects. Legal encyclopedias are organized by subject matter under *topics*, which are usually presented alphabetically in bound volumes. The commentary in an encyclopedia cites to statutes, cases, and rules, making it a one-stop shopping source for finding primary law.

Two encyclopedias exist for Georgia legal research. *Georgia Jurisprudence*, first published in 1996 and updated annually with pocket parts, brings together the cases, statutes, and rules that comprise the law on each topic. The *Encyclopedia of Georgia Law*, originally published in 1960, remains useful even though its last update occurred in 2002. When you are researching an issue governed by state law, you should start your research in a Georgia legal encyclopedia.

Table 8-4. Topics in *Georgia Jurisprudence*

Property (vols. 1–3)

Business and Commercial Law: Business Torts and Trade Regulation (vol. 4)

Business and Commercial Law: Uniform Commercial Code (vol. 5)

Business and Commercial Law: Corporations, Other Business Organizations and Securities Regulation (vol. 6)

Business and Commercial Law: Contracts (vol. 7)

Family Law (vol. 8)

Environmental Law (vol. 9)

Decedent's Estates and Trusts (vols. 10–11)

Workers' Compensation (vol. 12)

Personal Injury Torts (vols. 13–15)

Insurance (vol. 16)

Employment and Labor (vol. 17)

Criminal Law (vols. 20–22)

There are two national legal encyclopedias, *Corpus Juris Secundum* (C.J.S.) and *American Jurisprudence, Second Edition* (*Am. Jur. 2d*). These national encyclopedias serve well when you need general information or want to research the laws of other states.

A. *Georgia Jurisprudence*

Georgia Jurisprudence (*Ga. Jur.*), a West publication, is Georgia's state-specific encyclopedia. Unlike most other encyclopedias, the topics in *Ga. Jur.* are not arranged alphabetically. Instead, each topic has its own volume; several of the topics take up more than one volume. The topics are listed in Table 8-4.

Within the commentary of each topic, *Ga. Jur.* includes discussion of statutory, regulatory, and case law. Ample footnotes guide you to the primary sources. For this reason, finding your issue addressed in *Ga. Jur.* gives you a big step forward in your research.

To use *Georgia Jurisprudence*, start with either the General Index or the volume labeled "Finding Aids." You can find topics by subject in the General Index, which is located in two softbound volumes. The index will give you an abbreviation for the topic and the section number within it. Use the Table of Abbreviations in the front of the index to clarify the topic. In addition to the General Index, each topic contains an index of its own in the back of the volume.

The hardbound Finding Aids, volume 19, contains a Table of Cases, a Table of Statutes and Rules, and West's *Georgia Digest* conversion table. Use this volume to find sections which cite to cases, O.C.G.A. sections, Georgia court and bar rules, the *United States Code*, or the *Code of Federal Regulations*. The digest conversion table allows you to follow a search from the digest into the same subject in *Ga. Jur.*

You can find and use *Ga. Jur.* on Westlaw in the same way you would treatises. Using the Table of Contents feature allows you to browse or search a specific topic or section within a topic. Remember that you can book browse online in *Ga. Jur.* as well.

B. National Encyclopedias

In addition to the state encyclopedias, you may also want to use one of the national legal encyclopedias, *Corpus Juris Secundum* (C.J.S.) and *American Jurisprudence, Second Edition* (*Am. Jur. 2d*). The national encyclopedias are helpful when you are researching a federal issue, when you are researching a state issue that is not included in the Georgia encyclopedias, or when you want to know how other jurisdictions treat your issue.

To use a national encyclopedia in print, review its softbound index volumes for your research terms. The references will include both an abbreviated word or phrase—the topic—and a section number. The encyclopedia's topic abbreviations are explained in tables in the front of the index volumes. Select the bound volume containing a relevant topic. The spine of each volume includes the range of topics included in that volume.

To use an encyclopedia online, you can either do a Terms and Connectors search or browse the encyclopedia's table of contents. The table of contents for both national encyclopedias is long and detailed, so you may need to look under several topics before you find a section on point. On Westlaw, both encyclopedias are listed under "Forms, Treatises, CLEs, and Other Practice Material" in the directory. On LexisNexis, *Am. Jur. 2d* is available under "Secondary Legal > Jurisprudence & ALR" in the directory. C.J.S. is not available on LexisNexis.

Once you have found a relevant topic, skim the material at the beginning of that topic for an overview and general information. Online you can use the Table of Contents feature to see a topic outline. Once you have an overview of the topic, turn to the particular section number given in the index and read the text there.

The text of most encyclopedia entries is cursory because the goal of the writers is to summarize the law. Encyclopedia entries will identify any variations that exist between different jurisdictions, but they do not attempt to resolve differences or recommend improvements in the law. Most encyclopedias have annual pocket parts—additional pages inserted in the back of a volume—which provide more recent information than the commentary in the main volume. The encyclopedias online integrate these updates within the text, so you only have to look in one place.

Like *Georgia Jurisprudence*, the national encyclopedias include helpful footnotes accompanying the text. If a footnote refers to recent, primary authority from your jurisdiction, you will have made a great step forward in your research. However, because the footnotes in C.J.S. and *Am. Jur. 2d* cite to authorities from all American jurisdictions and tend to be dated, the chance of finding a reference to a recent, relevant case is limited. An encyclopedia's pocket parts may offer better prospects for researching primary authority. You can also Shepardize or KeyCite an older, relevant case to find more recent authority on point, or use the topics and key numbers given in a case from another jurisdiction to jump-start your research in your jurisdiction.

An encyclopedia may also contain cross-references to other sources. For example, C.J.S. includes cross-references to relevant topics and key numbers in West's digests. Similarly, *Am. Jur. 2d* cross-references *American Law Reports*, which are discussed later in this chapter.

V. Legal Periodicals

A. Law Reviews and Journals

Law reviews and law journals publish scholarly articles written by law professors, judges, practitioners, and law students. Each article explores in great detail a specific legal issue. Freed from the constraints of representing a client's interests or deciding a particular case, an author is able to explore whether the laws currently in force are the best legal rules and to propose changes.

Reading articles published in law reviews and law journals can give you a thorough understanding of current law because the authors often explain the existing law before making their recommendations. These articles may also identify weaknesses or new trends in the law that might address your client's situation. The many footnotes in law review and law journal articles can provide excellent summaries of relevant research.

Articles written by students are called "notes" or "comments." Although not as authoritative as articles written by recognized experts, student articles can provide clear and careful analysis, and their footnotes are valuable research tools.

Law reviews and law journals are generally published by law students who were selected according to grades or through a competition for membership on the editorial board. Most law reviews have general audiences and cover a broad range of topics. Examples include *Georgia Law Review*, *Yale Law Journal*, and *Stetson Law Review*. A growing number of other law journals focus on a specific area of law, for example, the *Journal of Environmental Law and Litigation* and *Columbia Journal of Transnational Law*. Table 8-5 lists law reviews and journals published by Georgia law schools.

Periodical issues are published in softbound booklets. Later, a library may bind the issues of a single volume together. The page numbers are consecutive throughout the volume, for example, an issue may have pages 584–1002. Citations to law review articles include the volume number, the name of the journal, and the first page of the article, for example, 96 Yale L.J. 1425 (1987).

**Table 8-5. Law Reviews and Journals Published
by Georgia Law Schools**

Emory Bankruptcy Developments Journal
Emory University School of Law
www.law.emory.edu/students/bdj

Emory International Law Review
Emory University School of Law
www.law.emory.edu/students/eilr

Emory Law Journal
Emory University School of Law
www.law.emory.edu/students/elj

Georgia Journal of International and Comparative Law
University of Georgia School of Law
www.law.uga.edu/gjicl

Georgia Law Review
University of Georgia School of Law
www.law.uga.edu/galawrev

Georgia State University Law Review
Georgia State University College of Law
http://law.gsu.edu/lawreview (contains annual Review of Selected
Georgia Legislation, which are also called "Peach Sheets")

Journal of Intellectual Property Law
University of Georgia School of Law
www.law.uga.edu/jipl

Journal of Southern Legal History
Mercer University School of Law
www.law.mercer.edu/academics/jslh

Mercer Law Review
Mercer University School of Law
www.law.mercer.edu/academics/lawreview (contains Annual Survey
of Georgia Law and annual Eleventh Circuit Survey)

Law review and law journal articles are not updated in the usual
sense, but you can find out whether an article has been cited favor-
ably or unfavorably by using the online updating services Shepard's
or KeyCite, or the print *Shepard's Law Review Citations*.

B. Bar Journals

Each state's bar journal contains articles of particular interest to attorneys practicing in that state. The State Bar of Georgia publishes useful articles in the *Georgia Bar Journal*. The American Bar Association (ABA) publishes the *ABA Journal* and other newsletters containing articles of general interest to attorneys across the nation.

Articles in bar journals are shorter than the articles published in law reviews and do not have the extensive footnotes found in law review articles. Moreover, the bar journal articles have a practitioner's focus. For example, the *Georgia Bar Journal* contains frequent articles on trends in law practice and firm management as well as articles analyzing recent court decisions.

C. Locating Articles

Researchers can use periodical indexes and full-text databases to find relevant articles. Using periodical indexes, researchers can focus on the articles that are on topic because they are indexed using a controlled list of subject headings. Using periodical indexes is often a more precise research method than searching journal articles in full-text databases.

A popular index of legal periodicals is the *Current Law Index* (CLI). Published by Thomson Gale, this index offers detailed subject indexing and covers international journals. The CLI is available in the online database LegalTrac, which is available at computer terminals in many libraries. The CLI is called "Legal Resource Index" on Westlaw (1980–present) and on LexisNexis (1977–present). You can find out more about the CLI on the Gale website at www.gale .com.

The *Current Index to Legal Periodicals* (CILP) is a weekly index published by the University of Washington Marian Gould Gallagher Law Library. It is available by subscription and also on Westlaw. Because it is more current than the other periodical indexes, you may want to use it when you are researching hot topics and current trends. The website for CILP is http://lib.law.washington.edu/cilp/ cilp.html.

An important print index for legal periodicals is the *Index to Legal Periodicals and Books* (ILPB), previously called the *Index to Legal Periodicals*. This index is especially useful in finding older articles because its coverage extends back to the early 1900s. ILPB indexes articles by both subject and author in a single alphabetical list. Thus, articles under the subject heading "Education" may be followed by an article under the author heading "Edwards, Linda Holdeman." ILPB volumes are published yearly. They are not cumulative, but are updated with softbound pamphlets. Monthly pamphlets are replaced periodically by quarterly pamphlets. These quarterly pamphlets stay on the shelves until the annual hardbound volume becomes available, sometimes several years later.

The ILPB is available online from the H.W. Wilson Company at www.hwwilson.com. In addition to ILPB, H.W. Wilson also offers *Index to Legal Periodicals Full Text* and *Index to Legal Periodicals Retrospective: 1908 to 1981*. The ILPB is also available on Westlaw from 1981 to the present and on LexisNexis from 1978 to the present.

Several online services include the full text of law reviews and other secondary sources. Full-text databases of law reviews are listed in the "Journals and Law Reviews" database on Westlaw and in the "U.S. Law Reviews and Journals, Combined" file on LexisNexis.

HeinOnline offers the full text of a large number of law review titles. Most law review articles are available on HeinOnline within a year or two of publication. A number of law school libraries subscribe to this service, which is available at www.heinonline.org. Because articles in HeinOnline are in portable document format (pdf), when you print an article it looks exactly as it would in the hard copy books. This is a big advantage over printing articles from Westlaw or Lexis-Nexis, which are not paginated like the books and which place footnotes at the end of documents.

Though HeinOnline offers full-text searching on its site, the search engine is not as sophisticated as that on Westlaw or LexisNexis. For this reason you will most often use HeinOnline to retrieve articles once you have the citations from an index.

VI. *American Law Reports*

Another valuable secondary source is the *American Law Reports* (ALR), where researchers find legal analysis of topics that include Georgia and other state law as well as federal law.

ALR offers both commentary on certain legal issues and the full text of published cases on those issues. The commentary articles are called *annotations*. They tend to focus on very narrow topics, take a practitioner's view, and provide a survey of the law in different jurisdictions. Thus, an annotation on the exact topic of your research is likely to be extremely helpful. Annotations are written by lawyers who are knowledgeable, but are not necessarily recognized experts. Each annotation is accompanied by a full-length case. This case may contain different editorial enhancements from those in a reporter, but the court's opinion will be exactly the same.

> EXAMPLE: In 1986, Congress passed the *Emergency Medical Treatment and Active Labor Act*, 42 U.S.C. § 1395dd (EMTALA). ALR reports a leading EMTALA case, *Thornton v. Southwest Detroit Hospital*, at 104 A.L.R. Fed. 157. The official cite for that case is 895 F.2d 1131. Following the *Thornton* case is an annotation, *Construction and Application of Emergency Medical Treatment and Active Labor Act (42 U.S.C.A. § 1395dd)*, written by a lawyer named Melissa K. Stull. Among some of the topics discussed in this annotation are the reasons Congress enacted EMTALA, the effect of related statutes, the liability imposed on hospitals, and available remedies.

There are several ALR series. Early series contained both state and federal subjects. Currently, federal subjects are included in *ALR Federal* and *ALR Federal 2d*. State subjects are discussed in numbered series: ALR 3d through ALR 6th.

To find annotations using the ALR in print, use the *ALR Quick Index*, which covers the third through the sixth series, or the *ALR Federal*

Quick Index. If you do not find your topic in the *Quick Index,* you can use the multi-volume *ALR Index* that covers the second through sixth series and the federal series. Remember that the older annotations are in the earlier series; when using the index, look for the annotations in the more recent series. The series also includes the multi-volume *West's ALR Digest,* which sets out the ALR cases in West's topic and key number arrangement. However, there is no reason to use this digest if you have access to West's *Federal Practice Digest* and West's *Georgia Digest* which are far more comprehensive. The value of the ALR series is the annotations, not the text of the cases.

ALR annotations are updated with pocket parts. You should also check the Annotation History Table in the index volumes to see whether an annotation has been supplemented or superseded by another annotation, rather than just updated.

You can also search for ALR annotations on Westlaw and Lexis-Nexis using Terms and Connectors or Natural Language searching. On Westlaw you can find ALRs in the "Forms, Treatises, CLEs, and Other Practice Material" directory; ALRs are in the "Secondary Legal" directory on LexisNexis.

VII. Treatises

A book on a legal topic can provide a deeper discussion and more relevant references than might be found in some other secondary sources. Legal texts include treatises, hornbooks, and Nutshells. All of these books share the purpose of covering a particular legal subject, such as contracts or civil procedure. They are distinguished mainly by their level of coverage. Treatises are generally considered to be more comprehensive statements on a subject than hornbooks, which offer a slightly more summarized view. Nutshells are a series of books published by West that offer an even more condensed explanation of law than hornbooks. Accordingly, an attorney may use a treatise to become familiar with a new area of legal practice, while a law student might typically turn to a hornbook or Nutshell to prepare for class, or later to gain a better understanding of a class lecture.

Treatises, hornbooks, and Nutshells can be located by using a library's catalog and searching for the general subject matter of your research project. After finding one book on point, scan the other titles shelved around it for additional resources.

To use a treatise or other book, begin with either the table of contents or the index. In multi-volume treatises, the index is often in the last volume of the series. Locate your research terms and record the references given. A reference will be to a page number, section number, or paragraph number, depending on the publisher. The table of contents or index should indicate which type of number is referenced. Turn to that part of the book, read the text, and note any pertinent primary authority cited in the footnotes.

Some treatises are so well known and widely respected that a colleague or supervisor may suggest that you begin research with a particular title. Examples include *Prosser & Keeton on the Law of Torts*, Wright & Miller's *Federal Practice and Procedure*, and Moore's *Federal Practice*. The first example covers the law of torts in one volume. The last two examples are multi-volume treatises.

Print treatises are updated in a variety of ways. Bound volumes like *Prosser & Keeton on the Law of Torts* and Wright & Miller's *Federal Practice and Procedure* (also available on Westlaw) are updated with pocket parts. Moore's *Federal Practice* (also available on LexisNexis) is published in loose-leaf binders, which are updated by replacing outdated pages throughout the binder with current material. Each page is dated to show when it was last updated. Also, new pages at the beginning of loose-leaf binders are often in different colors to draw the reader's attention. Nutshells are published in subsequent editions much more frequently than are treatises or hornbooks.

The authoritative value of a book depends largely on the reputation of the author. If the author is a widely recognized expert, his or her treatise may be cited by courts. In contrast, a Nutshell is designed as a study guide for students or a quick overview for practitioners, and it would not be considered authoritative.

Remember that both Westlaw and LexisNexis offer treatises online. Westlaw treatises, other than Nutshells and most hornbooks, can be found in the "Treatises, CLEs, Practice Guides" section of the directory, and LexisNexis treatises are listed by publisher (i.e., Matthew Bender, Aspen, John Wiley, etc.) under "Secondary Legal."

VIII. Mini-Libraries and Loose-Leaf Services

A *mini-library* combines both primary and secondary sources under one title. In areas of law like taxation and environmental law, a single title may contain statutes, administrative regulations, annotations to cases and agency opinions, and commentary. The benefit is obvious: all of the material is gathered together so that you do not have to consult multiple sources.

A. Print Resources

In print, a topical mini-library is often referred to as a loose-leaf service. This is because the pages are kept in loose-leaf, three-ring binders instead of being bound as books. The loose-leaf format allows the publisher to send updates frequently and quickly; the outdated pages are removed and the new pages inserted on a regular basis. A loose-leaf service generally fills numerous volumes. The volumes may be arranged by topic, by statute, or by another system.

Loose-leaf services always have a "How to Use" section, generally near the beginning of the first volume. You should review this section before starting your research. You may also want to skim through a few volumes to become familiar with the organization of that particular service. Pay careful attention to each service's method and frequency of updating.

How you use a loose-leaf service depends on what you know at the beginning of your research. In tax research, for example, if you need to look up a particular section of the Internal Revenue Code (IRC), go to the *Standard Federal Tax Reporter*, and find the volume whose spine indicates that your IRC section is included. Turning to that section, you would find the statutory language, followed by regulations issued by the Treasury Department. Next, you would see annotations to cases decided by courts of general jurisdiction as well as by the U.S. Tax Court. Also included would be rulings of the Internal Revenue Service. At the end of coverage of that section of the IRC, you would find commentary written by the publisher.

If you do not know the particular section of a loose-leaf that you need to research, begin with the topical index. Often this is the first or last volume of the series. Look up your research terms, and write down the reference numbers given. These will likely be paragraph numbers rather than page numbers. To maintain indexing despite frequent updates, loose-leaf services often are organized by paragraph number. A "paragraph" may be just a few sentences, several actual paragraphs, or many pages in length. Even though the page numbers will change with future updates, the paragraph reference will remain constant.

Turn to each paragraph number referenced in the index under your research terms. Realize that the paragraph number may be for the statute, regulations, annotations, or commentary. Turn to earlier and later pages around that paragraph number to ensure that you have reviewed all relevant material.

B. Online Services

Loose-leaf services are now available online from major publishers such as BNA and CCH. These services provide full-text searching in addition to the index searching explained above. For example, CCH provides the *Standard Federal Tax Reporter* to subscribers in an online database called CCH Tax Research Network. Usually you can view an online tutorial to learn to use the product in an electronic format. Some products allow you to create a research trail and remember the query words and results you get; printing these will help you keep track of your research easily.

In addition to loose-leaf services, the publisher BNA offers a plethora of topical newsletters online. Many law libraries subscribe to the online newsletters and make them available to their students on in-house computers. Some of the topics covered in the newsletters are criminal law, environmental law, trade regulation, and labor law. The expert writers at BNA are highly regarded in the legal profession. The strength of the newsletters is currency; use them to get the latest information on hot topics and up-to-date information on many areas of law.

IX. Forms

A form can be a great shortcut in drafting a legal document, especially a document you are drafting for the first time in an unfamiliar area of law. A form provides an excellent starting point by keeping you from reinventing the wheel.

Take care in using any form. Forms are designed for general audiences, not your particular client. Before using a form, ensure that you understand every word in the form and modify it to suit your client's needs. Do not simply fill in the blanks and assume that the form correctly represents your client's position. Unless a particular form is prescribed by statute or by a court, revise the wording to avoid unnecessary legalese.

Forms are available in diverse sources. Georgia statutes provide forms for some particular situations. For example, O.C.G.A. § 9-11-109 contains a form of complaint for negligence, O.C.G.A. § 19-12-3 contains a change-of-name form, and O.G.C.A. § 19-8-26 contains forms for surrender of parental rights during an adoption. To find statutory forms, search the O.C.G.A. general index both for the substantive content of the form and under the term "forms."

Forms may also be found in court rules (discussed in Chapter 4) and CLE materials (discussed in Part III of this chapter). A "formbook" may provide actual forms or suggested language that can be crafted into a form. You can find a list of Georgia formbooks on a variety of legal topics in the bibliography in Appendix C at the end of this book.

Federal forms are available in numerous titles, including *West's Federal Forms* and *American Jurisprudence Legal Forms 2d*. Search the library catalog by subject for topical formbooks.

The Georgia Administrative Office of the Courts provides a number of forms at www.georgiacourts.org/forms.html#pof. The website has a variety of forms in the area of family law as well as inmate forms. The websites of counties or other courts may contain additional forms. For example, the Dougherty County Law Library provides links to a variety of forms online at www.dougherty .ga.us/law_library/LL_index.htm, and the Fulton County Superior Court website includes domestic relations forms at www.fulton court.org/family/adobe.php. The Mercer Law School Library website contains links to Georgia forms online at www.law.mercer.edu/ library/GeorgiaResources/GeorgiaResources.cfm (click on "Legal Forms").

X. Restatements

A restatement is an organized and detailed summary of the common law in a specific legal area. Familiar titles include *Restatement of the Law of Contracts* and *Restatement of the Law of Torts*. Restatements are the results of collaborative efforts by committees of scholars, practitioners, and judges organized by the American Law Institute (ALI). These committees, led by a scholar called the *reporter*, draft text that explains the common law in rule format (i.e., they are written with outline headings similar to statutes, rather than in the narrative form of cases). The committees circulate the drafts for review and revision. The restatement that is published by ALI includes not only the text of the rules that embody the common law but also commentary, illustrations, and notes from the reporter.

Restatements were originally intended simply to restate the law as it existed, in an effort to build national consistency in key common law areas. Over time, restatements grew more aggressive in stating what the authors thought the law should be.

A portion of a restatement becomes primary authority only if it is adopted by a court in a particular case. After a court has adopted a portion of a restatement, the committee's commentary and illustrations, as well as any notes provided by the reporter, may be valuable tools in interpreting the restatement. Cases in other jurisdictions that have adopted the restatement become persuasive authority.

To find a relevant restatement, search the library catalog for the subject matter or search for the word "restatement" in the title of a book. Within each restatement, use the table of contents or index to find pertinent sections. The text of each restatement section is followed by commentary and sometimes illustrations of key points made in the text. Appendix volumes list citations to cases that have referred to the restatement.

Restatements are also available on Westlaw in the "ALI Restatements of the Law & Principles of the Law" folder under the directory heading "Forms, Treatises, CLEs, and Other Practice Material" and on LexisNexis in the "Secondary Legal > Restatements of the Law" section of the directory. To use the restatements online, you can either use a Terms and Connectors search or browse the table of contents.

The text of a restatement is updated only when a later version is published. However, the appendix volumes are updated with pocket parts or softbound supplements, and online sources continually add more recent information. Shepardizing or KeyCiting a restatement section will reveal cases and articles that cite the restatement. Remember that you can limit your Shepard's or KeyCite display to Georgia cases to find out if the courts have adopted a section of a restatement.

XI. Jury Instructions

Pattern jury instructions provide uniform instructions for juries in civil and criminal trials. By examining the instructions in advance of trial, an attorney may better be able to present evidence to the jury. Even if a case ends before trial, knowing the instructions a jury would receive may produce more effective research. The Council of Superior Court Judges of Georgia publishes *Suggested Pattern Jury Instructions* in loose-leaf binders. Volume 1 is Civil Cases 4th edition, and volume 2 is Criminal Cases 3d edition. To use the jury instructions, browse the table of contents for your research terms or consult the index (in the criminal volume).

You can also find federal jury instructions in publications such as O'Malley, Grenig, & Lee, *Federal Jury Practice and Instructions.* In addition, West publishes softbound volumes for each federal circuit for both civil and criminal instructions, for example, *Eleventh Circuit Pattern Jury Instructions, Civil.* You can find these in a library catalog by searching for "pattern jury instructions" or "model jury instructions" in the title of the book. Though these books do not have an index, they have detailed tables of contents.

XII. Using Secondary Sources and Practice Aids in Research

As the above discussions suggest, which source you use will depend on your research project. For a broad overview, an encyclopedia may be best. For in-depth analysis on a narrow topic, an article is more likely to be helpful. On cutting-edge issues, CLE material often covers new areas of law quickly. In litigation, court-approved forms and uniform jury instructions will be indispensable.

Consider your own background in the subject matter and the goals of your research, and select from these sources accordingly. A source that was not helpful in your last research project may be perfect for the current project. How many secondary sources you use depends on the success of your early searches and the time available to you. It would almost never be prudent to check every source discussed in this chapter.

Despite the value of secondary sources, rarely will you cite a secondary source in writing a memorandum or brief. Some sources, such as indexes for finding periodicals, are not "authority" at all. Rather, they are finding tools and should never be cited. Encyclopedias, ALR annotations, and CLE material should be cited only as a last resort. Even sources that are secondary authority, including law review articles and treatises, should be cited infrequently. Instead, cite to primary authority.

Three exceptions exist. First, sometimes you need to summarize the development of the law. If no case has provided that summary, citing a treatise or law review article that traces that development could be helpful to your reader. Citation to secondary authority is also appropriate when there is no law on point for an argument you are making. This is likely to occur with new issues. It may also occur when you are arguing to expand or change the law. In these situations, your only support may come from a law review article. Finally, secondary authority may provide additional support for a point cited to primary authority. For example, you can bolster an argument supported by a case, especially if it is from another jurisdiction, by also citing an article or treatise by a respected expert on the topic.

Whether or not you cite a secondary source in a document, you must decide the weight to give secondary authority in developing your own analysis. Consider the following criteria:

Who is the author? The views of a respected scholar, an acknowledged expert, or a judge carry more weight than a student author or an anonymous editor.

When was the material published? Especially for cutting-edge issues, a more recent article is likely to be more helpful. Even with more traditional issues, be sure that the material analyzes the current state of the law.

Where was the material published? Articles published in established law journals are generally granted the most respect. A school's prestige and the length of the journal's existence influence how well established a journal is. Thus, a journal that has been published for a century at a top law school will carry more respect than a journal at a new, unaccredited school. A publication specific to your jurisdiction or dedicated to a particular topic, however, may be more helpful than a publication from another state or one with a general focus.

What depth is provided? The more focused and thorough the analysis, the more useful the material will be.

How relevant is it to your argument? If the author is arguing your exact point, the material will be more persuasive than if the author's arguments are only tangential to yours.

Has this secondary source been cited previously by courts? If a court has found an article persuasive in the past, it is likely to find it persuasive again. Remember that the text of a secondary source may become primary authority if it is adopted by a court or legislature.

Appendix 8-A. Online Sources of
Georgia Secondary Source Materials

CARL VINSON INSTITUTE OF GOVERNMENT, UNIVERSITY OF GEORGIA — Free www.cviog.uga.edu		
Content	Publishes a variety of titles useful to attorneys	
Notes	See the Public Policy Research Series at www.cviog.uga.edu/pprs, which includes Policy Papers and Notes	

CASEMAKER — Free to members of the State Bar of Georgia www.gabar.org	
Content	*Georgia Bar Journal* and *Georgia State University Law Review*
Coverage	*Georgia Bar Journal* (selected articles from August 2000 to present) *Georgia State University Law Review* (Fall 2000–present)

FAMILY DIVISION OF THE SUPERIOR COURT OF FULTON COUNTY — Free http://www.fultoncourt.org/family	
Content	Helpful tips and forms

FULTON COUNTY LAW LIBRARY (ATLANTA) — Free http://www.fultoncourt.org/lawlibrary	
Content	Helpful tips and forms

HEINONLINE — Commercial www.heinonline.org	
Content	Full-text law reviews
Coverage	Depends on title; most start with volume 1 of the journal

LEXISNEXIS — Commercial www.lexis.com	
Content	Full-text law reviews, treatises, and periodical indexes
Coverage	Depends on title

STATE OF GEORGIA, OFFICIAL WEBSITE — Free www.georgia.gov	
Content	Variety of legal and non-legal information

WESTLAW — Commercial www.westlaw.com	
Content	Full-text law reviews, treatises, and periodical indexes
Coverage	Depends on title

Chapter 9

Legal Ethics Research

After reading this chapter you will:
- be familiar with the historical development of professional ethics in the U.S.; and
- understand the steps and resources needed to perform thorough legal ethics research.

I. Introduction to Legal Ethics Research

Having the skills necessary to research legal ethics issues will benefit anyone in the legal profession on more occasions than expected. For example, are there exceptions to the attorney-client privilege? Are you asking your legal assistant to perform the duties of a lawyer? What duties are owed to your former clients?

Earlier chapters addressed locating cases, statutes, administrative rules, and secondary sources. This chapter applies the skills from those chapters to locate relevant cases, statutes, and their counterparts such as model rules, ethics opinions, disciplinary proceedings, and commentary. Pieced together, these relevant sources will provide answers to a legal ethics issue.

Unlike other chapters in this book where state and federal resources are considered separately, the process of researching a Georgia ethics issue may naturally include resources from jurisdictions outside of Georgia, and, therefore, must be considered in the research steps if applicable. Typically, resources from other jurisdictions are considered when there is not enough Georgia precedent. American Bar Association (ABA) resources, for example, are considered the nationwide equivalent to Georgia Bar Association resources and can be persuasive in Georgia courts when Georgia precedent is lacking. Consequently, the process of doing state-level ethics research may reach beyond the bounds of state resources.

II. The Model Rules: A Brief History

The ABA has adopted many versions of rules governing conduct in the legal profession. Table 9-1 provides a timeline of the development of rules regulating attorney conduct.

**Table 9-1. Timeline of Historical Development of
Rules of Professional Ethics (U.S.)**

1836   David Hoffman, founder of University of Maryland Law School, wrote fifty *Resolutions in Regard to Professional Development* for his students

1854   Honorable George Sharswood, professor of law at University of Pennsylvania, published *A Compend[ium] of Lectures on the Aims and Duties of the Profession of Law*

1887   David Goode Jones, an Alabama attorney, provided leadership that led to the adoption of the *Code of Ethics* by the Alabama Bar Association

1908   The American Bar Association adopted the *Canons of Professional Ethics*

1969   The Special Committee on Evaluation of Ethical Standards produced, and the ABA adopted, the *Model Code of Professional Responsibility* (Model Code)

1977   ABA Commission on Evaluation of Professional Standards (Kutak Commission) formed

1983   ABA House of Delegates adopted the *Model Rules of Professional Conduct* (Model Rules)

1997   ABA's Ethics 2000 Commission began writing new rules to address current issues; subsequently, most remaining Model Code states adopted all or part of the Model Rules

Most notably, the ABA adopted the *Model Code of Professional Responsibility* (Model Code) in 1969 and, in 1983, the ABA subsequently adopted the *Model Rules of Professional Conduct* (Model Rules) and has revised them many times. To date, about forty-five states, including Georgia, have abandoned the Model Code and adopted the Model Rules in whole or in part.

The Model Rules are ideal professional standards set forth by the ABA. Like model laws, they are not binding in a jurisdiction until adopted by the legislature, the supreme court, or the bar association of the jurisdiction. Georgia's Supreme Court adopted the ABA's Model Rules on June 12, 2000. These rules, which became effective on January 1, 2001, are called the *Georgia Rules of Professional Conduct* (GRPC). The GRPC vary slightly from the true form of the ABA's Model Rules, but they are in the same spirit. The *American Bar Association/Bureau of National Affairs (ABA/BNA) Lawyers' Manual on Professional Conduct*, Ethics Rules Library, contains *State Variations of ABA Rules*, located at www.bna.com. This resource compares the differences between the ABA Model Rules and the GRPC.

III. Legal Ethics Research: Organize the Process

Legal ethics research involves pulling together many different primary and secondary resources, beginning at the state level. Table 9-2 is a basic checklist you can use to organize the research steps.

A. Preparation for Research

Steps 1 through 3 are preparation for your research. First, list the parties involved. Next, list all of the legal issues in your research problem in keyword or short phrase form. These keywords become your initial search terms in a print index or online database throughout

Table 9-2. Legal Ethics Research Steps

Step 1	List the parties involved.
Step 2	List the issues in keyword or short phrase form.
Step 3	List all jurisdictions that could apply to your research problem.
Step 4	Search Georgia rules and their equivalent counterparts.
Step 5	Search Georgia case law and its equivalent counterparts.
Step 6	Assess whether your research is complete. If your research is not complete, proceed to Step 7.
Step 7	Seek resources from the ABA; if none, seek resources from other states as last resort precedent.
Step 8	Consult relevant secondary sources.

the research process. Typically, legal ethics research takes place at the state level. Does the ethics issue at hand involve more than one state? List all jurisdictions that could apply.

B. Georgia Rules

Begin Step 4 by seeking relevant rules from the *Georgia Rules of Professional Conduct* (GRPC). The Georgia Supreme Court adopted the GRPC and integrated them into its court rules.

There are many print resources that include the text of the GRPC including *ABA/BNA Lawyers' Manual on Professional Conduct, Georgia Court Manual Rules and Regulations Annotated, Georgia Court Rules and Procedure—State and Federal,* and *Georgia Rules of Court Annotated.* The print *State Bar of Georgia Directory & Handbook,* published annually in November as a special supplement to the *Georgia Bar Journal,* also includes the text of the GRPC. *West's Code of Georgia Annotated* includes the GRPC in the second volume of state court rules. Online sources of the GRPC are listed in Table 9-3, with expanded information in Appendix 9-A.

**Table 9-3. Online Sources Containing the Georgia Rules
of Professional Conduct**

Current Rules (2001–present)	Web Address	Free or Commercial
Bureau of National Affairs	www.bna.com	Commercial
LexisNexis	www.lexis.com	Commercial
Loislaw	www.loislaw.com	Commercial
State Bar of Georgia	www.gabar.org/ethics/ethics__ discipline_rules	Free
Westlaw	www.westlaw.com	Commercial

Separate rules exist to govern judicial conduct in Georgia. The *Georgia Code of Judicial Conduct* is available online on LexisNexis, Westlaw, the *ABA/BNA Lawyers' Manual,* and the State Bar of Georgia's website.[1] Rules governing judicial conduct are also available in the following print resources: *Georgia Court Manual Rules and Regulations Annotated, Georgia Court Rules and Procedure—State and Federal, Georgia Rules of Court Annotated,* and *West's Code of Georgia Annotated.*

The research process for locating relevant sections of the GRPC online requires using the keywords created in the legal ethics checklist. In LexisNexis, Westlaw, and Loislaw, use these keywords to search in the appropriate database. The State Bar's search capability, on the other hand, consists of a Google-driven search of the entire State Bar website.

After locating relevant rules from the GRPC, seek relevant Georgia statutes. Using your keywords and the information in Chapter 4 of this book, consult the print index or search online in the *Official Code of Georgia Annotated* or *West's Code of Georgia Annotated* for relevant statutes. In most cases, there won't be a statute on point; however, ruling out this possibility is necessary for thorough research.

---

1. The *Georgia Code of Judicial Conduct* via the State Bar of Georgia website is available at www.gabar.org/handbook/georgia_code_of_judicial_ conduct.

Refer to Table 4-6 for a list of online sources that can be used to access the Georgia code.

C. Georgia Case Law

In Step 5, seek Georgia case law and its legal ethics counterparts such as Georgia advisory opinions, results of disciplinary proceedings, and other documents that have precedential value. Relevant Georgia case law may be a useful resource. To locate cases you can either use a print or an online digest or a case law database. Refer back to Chapter 3 for the process of doing a print or online digest search.

1. Advisory Opinions

The Formal Advisory Opinion Board of the State Bar of Georgia drafts formal advisory opinions that the Georgia Supreme Court approves, disapproves, or modifies. The weight of the opinion depends on its treatment by the Court.[2] Formal advisory opinions address questions of general interest. For example, lawyer advertising is a topic of general interest and is addressed in Formal Advisory Opinion 92-2 (July 30, 1992). An image of a selected portion of Formal Advisory Opinion 92-2 is available in Table 9-4. Informal advisory opinions address a specific set of facts and may be issued orally or in writing.[3]

Prior to 1986, the State Disciplinary Board drafted the advisory opinions. Use these older opinions with caution if the Supreme Court of Georgia did not subsequently adopt the opinion. These opinions are still available on the State Bar of Georgia Disciplinary Board Opinions website at www.gabar.org/handbook/state_disciplinary_board _opinions.

The *National Reporter on Legal Ethics & Professional Responsibility*, published by LexisNexis, makes available in print and online advisory

---

2. *See* State Bar of Georgia, Rule 4-403, Formal Advisory Opinions, available at www.gabar.org/handbook/rule_4-403_formal_advisory_opinions.
3. *See* State Bar of Georgia, Rule 4-401, Informal Advisory Opinions, available at www.gabar.org/handbook/rule_4-401_informal_advisory_opinions.

Table 9-4. Image of Selected Portion of Formal Advisory Opinion 92-2 (July 30, 1992)

Ethical propriety of a lawyer advertising for legal business with the intention of referring a majority of that business out to other lawyers without disclosing that intent in the advertisement.

It is ethically improper for a lawyer to advertise for legal business with the intention of referring a majority of that business out to other lawyers without disclosing that intent in the advertisement and without complying with the disciplinary standards of conduct applicable to lawyer referral services.

Correspondent seeks ethical advice for a practicing attorney who advertises legal services, but whose ads do not disclose that a majority of the responding callers will be referred to other lawyers. The issue is whether the failure to include information about the lawyers referral practices in the ad is misleading in violation of the State Bar of Georgia Standards of Conduct and Directory Rules.

Standard 5 of Rule 4-102, governing advertising of legal services, prohibits a lawyer from making "any false, fraudulent, deceptive, or misleading communication about the lawyer or the lawyer's services." A communication is false or misleading if it "[c]ontains a material misrepresentation of fact or law, or omits a fact necessary to make the statement considered as a whole not materially misleading," Standard 5(A)(1).

The advertisement of legal services is protected commercial speech under the First Amendment. Bates v. State Bar of Arizona, 433 U.S. 350(1977). Commercial speech ". . . serves to inform the public of the availability, nature, and prices of products and services.

Table 9-5. Sources of Advisory Opinions and
Disciplinary Board Proceedings Online

Source	Advisory Opinions or Disciplinary Board Proceedings	Web Address	Free or Commercial
LexisNexis	Advisory Opinions	www.lexis.com	Commercial
State Bar of Georgia Website	Both	www.gabar.org/ethics/ advisory_opinions	Free
Westlaw	Advisory Opinions	www.westlaw.com	Commercial

opinions for every state. Advisory opinions can also be retrieved online through LexisNexis, Westlaw, and the State Bar of Georgia website. To locate relevant advisory opinions online, run searches using the keywords created in the legal ethics checklist.

2. Disciplinary Proceedings

In addition to advisory opinions, use your keywords to explore the results of disciplinary proceedings, which may provide some relevant precedent. Disciplinary proceedings are available on the State Bar of Georgia website from 1986 to the present.

Table 9-5 lists online sources that provide access to advisory opinions and disciplinary proceedings. More detailed information is provided in Appendix 9-B.

D. Precedent from Other Jurisdictions and Secondary Sources

Steps 7 and 8 are optional and should be explored if your research is not complete at this point. Your research is complete if you have enough Georgia sources to address your legal issue. If your research does not seem complete, try the following sources.

Precedent from other jurisdictions may hold weight in Georgia courts when Georgia precedent is lacking. Using your keywords, consult statutory and case law resources and their counterparts from the

ABA. As a last resort, precedent from other jurisdictions may be pursued for guidance, although there is no guarantee that Georgia courts will consider precedent from other states persuasive.

Secondary sources are another excellent resource. Consult resources such as the *Restatement of the Law: The Law Governing Lawyers, 3d*; law review articles; and other sources of commentary.

The *Restatement of the Law: The Law Governing Lawyers*, a secondary source available in print and online, contains black letter law and commentary about ethical issues pertaining to attorney conduct. Use your keywords to search the print index or online in LexisNexis or Westlaw. Refer to Chapter 8 of this book for the availability of additional online secondary sources.

Law review articles and treatises are additional secondary sources for legal ethics research. Locate law review articles by using your keywords in the *Index to Legal Periodicals* or *Current Law Index* in print or online. In addition, LexisNexis and Westlaw's law review databases and HeinOnline's Law Journal Library contain the full text of law review articles.

Table 9-6 lists online sources to access precedent from other jurisdictions. Appendix 9-C expands this information and provides additional information about secondary sources.

Table 9-6. Precedent from Other Jurisdictions Available Online

Source	Web Address	Free or Commercial
ABA Center for Professional Ethics	www.abanet.org/cpr/center_entities.html	Free
LexisNexis	www.lexis.com	Commercial
National Organization of Bar Counsel	http://nobc.org/cases/cotm.asp	Free
Westlaw	www.westlaw.com	Commercial

Appendix 9-A. Sources of Georgia Rules of Professional Conduct (GRPC) Online

BUREAU OF NATIONAL AFFAIRS (BNA) — Commercial www.bna.com	
Content	*ABA/BNA Lawyer's Manual on Professional Conduct*
Coverage	Current version of GRPC
Update	Updated as received from the Georgia Supreme Court
LEXISNEXIS — Commercial www.lexis.com	
Content	*Georgia Rules of Professional Conduct*
Coverage	Current version of GRPC
Update	Updated as received from the Georgia Supreme Court
LOISLAW — Commercial www.loislaw.com	
Content	*Georgia Rules of Professional Conduct*
Coverage	Current version of GRPC
Update	Updated as received from the Georgia Supreme Court
STATE BAR OF GEORGIA — Free www.gabar.org/ethics/ethics__discipline_rules	
Content	*Georgia Rules of Professional Conduct*
Coverage	Current rules (2001–present) Old rules (prior to 2001)
Update	Updated as new rules are adopted from the Georgia Supreme Court
WESTLAW — Commercial www.westlaw.com	
Content	*Georgia Rules of Court*
Coverage	Current version of the GRPC
Update	Updated as received from the Georgia Supreme Court

Appendix 9-B. Sources of Ethics Cases, Advisory Opinions, and Disciplinary Proceedings Online

LEXISNEXIS — Commercial www.lexis.com	
Content	Georgia state case law and ethics opinions
Coverage	Current
Update	Updated within 24–48 hours of receipt

LEXISNEXIS — Commercial www.lexis.com	
Content	*National Reporter on Legal Ethics and Professional Responsibility*
Coverage	Selected formal and informal ethics opinions 1991–present
Update	Updated when received from vendor
Notes	Database includes all fifty states; limit to Georgia by using the following segment search: STATE(Georgia)

STATE BAR OF GEORGIA — Free www.gabar.org/ethics/advisory_opinions/	
Content	Advisory Opinions
Coverage	Formal Advisory Opinions (1986–present)
Update	Updated as issued by the Supreme Court of Georgia

STATE BAR OF GEORGIA — Free www.gabar.org/handbook/state_disciplinary_board_opinions/	
Content	State Disciplinary Board Opinions
Coverage	Current advisory opinions (1986–present)
Update	Updated as issued by the Supreme Court of Georgia

WESTLAW — Commercial www.westlaw.com	
Content	Georgia Legal Ethics and Professional Responsibility Cases
Coverage	1846–present
Update	Updated as cases become available

Appendix 9-C. Precedent from Other Jurisdictions and Secondary Sources Online

AMERICAN BAR ASSOCIATION CENTER FOR PROFESSIONAL ETHICS — Free www.abanet.org/cpr/center_entities.html	
Content	Miscellaneous lawyer regulation resources
Coverage	Varies depending on the resource
Update	Schedule unknown
Notes	Contains the full text of the Model Rules of Professional Conduct available at www.abanet.org/cpr/mrpc/mrpc_home.html

LEXISNEXIS — Commercial www.lexis.com	
Content	*ABA/BNA Lawyers' Manual on Professional Conduct*
Coverage	Current
Update	When received from BNA

LEXISNEXIS — Commercial www.lexis.com	
Content	*Restatement of the Law — The Law Governing Lawyers*
Coverage	Current restatement
Update	As received from the publisher
Notes	LexisNexis features an Annotated Case Citations database that includes Annotations to Restatement Rules and Notes (updated annually) and the ALI's Interim Case Citations (updated two times per year)

NATIONAL ORGANIZATION OF BAR COUNSEL — Free http://nobc.org/cases/cotm.asp	
Content	Cases of the Month — Featured disciplinary proceedings
Coverage	Selected disciplinary proceedings from all jurisdictions
Update	Monthly

WESTLAW — Commercial www.westlaw.com	
Content	Legal Ethics & Professional Responsibility — American Bar Association Ethics Opinions
Coverage	Formal opinions (January 1924–present) Informal opinions (July 1961–present)
Update	As new opinions are received from the ABA

Appendix 9-C. Precedent from Other Jurisdictions and Secondary Sources Online, cont'd

WESTLAW — Commercial www.westlaw.com	
Content	*Restatement of the Law — The Law Governing Lawyers*
Coverage	Current
Update	Three times per year
Notes	Westlaw also features a companion archive database that features all drafts of this restatement from Tentative Draft No. 1, 1998, to the present
WESTLAW — Commercial www.westlaw.com	
Content	*ABA/BNA Lawyer's Manual on Professional Conduct*
Coverage	Ethics Opinions (1986–present)
Update	As received from publisher

Chapter 10

Online Legal Research

After reading this chapter you will be able to:

- decide whether to begin your research in print or online sources;
- assess websites for authoritativeness, completeness, currency, and general usefulness;
- seek out low-cost, reliable online sources for legal research; and
- locate help screens that will introduce you to search techniques specific to the commercial database or website you are searching.

I. Integrating Print and Online Research

Developing a comprehensive research strategy includes deciding when and how to use print and online resources. It also means being realistic about what is available online. While it may be possible to do thorough research using only online sources, be prepared to dabble in the print resources also.

Online resources include commercial providers like LexisNexis and Westlaw. Their databases contain enormous numbers of documents, and their complex search engines enable the researcher to craft detailed requests. Free online resources maintained by government entities, universities, and law schools provide an increasing number of legal documents. General search engines like Google and websites with non-legal information may be helpful resources as well.

II. Choosing Print or Online Sources

Online research has a number of advantages. Most significant among these are the ease of searching, the convenience of downloading or printing important documents, and the frequency with which many online sources are updated. Nevertheless, online searching is not always the most effective or cost-efficient way to conduct your research; even fans of online research agree that *beginning* research with books, whether primary or secondary sources, is often more productive than beginning online. Consider the following factors when choosing print or online:

Authorship. Can you verify the author and his reputation?

Citation. Does the source provide the information needed for proper citation? For example, some online sources do not provide pagination. In addition, some citation schemes, such as the *Bluebook*, require you to cite to the date on the volume or pocket part. Online sources do not provide this information.

Completeness. Are you under the impression that everything is online? Unfortunately, this is not true and you may be overlooking some key print resources.

Cost. Do you have unlimited resources at your disposal or are you on a budget? Is the source free? If it will cost you or your client money, have you considered low-cost or free alternatives?

Currency. How current is the source? When was the last time the source was updated?

Efficiency. Are you more comfortable doing research in one format? Are you familiar with Terms and Connectors or Natural Language searching? Do you know the difference between the searches both "behind the scenes" and in the results that are displayed? Are you familiar with segment or field searching?

Subject. Are you familiar with the area of law you are researching? Familiarity may lend itself to an online search, while unfamiliarity may lend itself better to print research with a keyword index and cross-references.

Is the area of law new or emerging? New or unique terminology in emerging areas may be easier to find online. In addition, the scarcity of resources on emerging topics may mean you are more successful performing full-text searches.

III. Online Sources for Legal Research

It is common for legal researchers to find the same material available on multiple websites or through multiple commercial databases. You must evaluate the reliability, accessibility, cost, and currency, among other factors, when choosing the best source for the information you need.

A. Commercial Providers

LexisNexis and Westlaw are the largest commercial providers of computerized legal research. Both have reputations for accurate material and user-friendly search techniques. They provide extensive coverage of primary and secondary authority. Bureau of National Affairs (BNA) is also a leading provider of online legal information.

Other commercial providers of legal materials include Casemaker, Fastcase, Loislaw, and VersusLaw. They tend to be less expensive than LexisNexis, Westlaw, and BNA, but they also provide less extensive coverage.

Many commercial online vendors are embracing the trend of providing digitized documents or some form of mirror-image of the print publication. Typically more pleasing to the eye than text versions, digitized materials also offer access to page breaks that are needed to conform with most standard rules of citation.

Table 10-1. Selected Sources of Primary Authority
from the State of Georgia

Primary Authority	State of Georgia Website
Georgia Constitution	www.sos.state.ga.us/elections/constitution.htm
Official Code of Georgia Annotated	http://w3.lexis-nexis.com/hottopics/gacode/Default.asp?
Rules and Regulations of the State of Georgia	www.sos.state.ga.us/rules_regs.htm

B. Government and University Websites

Government entities and universities often provide access to their website information for free. These websites contain less information than is available from the commercial providers, and the search engines on these websites tend to be more primitive. However, the information available on these websites is considered very reliable and is increasing, making them more useful research tools. Also, because they are free, they are worth exploring.

Many libraries contain links to valuable websites, even when the library itself does not maintain the material. Some examples are Cornell Law School's Legal Information Institute at www.law.cornell.edu, Washburn University School of Law's "WashLaw" at www.washlaw.edu, and the Law Library of Congress Guide to Law Online for U.S. States and Territories at www.loc.gov/law/guide/us-ga.html. The Georgia segments of those websites list links to Georgia cases, statutes, administrative material, and more. A similar "gateway" website is FindLaw at www.findlaw.com, which was recently purchased by West but remains a free resource. The "For Legal Professionals" tab provides a "Jurisdiction" link (under "Research the Law"), and then a "Georgia" link.

Like other states, Georgia maintains its own websites for its primary authority. Although the print versions are the "official" authority, the online versions are useful for research. Table 10-1 provides a selected list of Georgia's primary authority websites. In addition, a number of Georgia law school libraries maintain websites that provide reliable, though limited, information. Emory University Law Library maintains a website linking to Georgia primary authority at www.law.emory.edu/index.php?id=4242.

C. Other Websites

A new trend among law firms is to provide legal information to clients on firm websites. One example is Alston & Bird's International Privacy Resource Center at http://resource.alston.com/abResource-Center/resource_overview.aspx?s=3. This library provides links to related U.S. laws, multilateral instruments, European Union directives, country links, and advisories.

Outside the realm of commercial, university, government, and law firm websites is a vast array of other websites that may or may not provide accurate information. A keen researcher will evaluate the website to determine if it provides accurate, authoritative, reliable information.

IV. Online Search Techniques

Internet search engines allow their users to locate websites on a given topic. Search engines such as Yahoo!, Google, and Ask.com provide a choice between using basic or advanced search techniques. On Internet search engines, the basic search is essentially a Natural-Language or free-text search. Table 10-2 is an image of the Yahoo! basic search page. A search for the phrase "unauthorized practice of law" returned an overwhelming 191,000 websites. Table 10-3 shows the search results.

Search engine users can take advantage of advanced search capabilities to narrow the results. Table 10-4 is an image of the Yahoo! advanced search page with the exact search phrase "unauthorized practice of law" and then any of the keywords "attorney," "lawyer," or "counselor." In addition, the search results can be limited to websites that have been updated within the past year. This more advanced search still returned an overwhelming 1,620 websites as shown in Table 10-5. Adding more restrictions or keywords will allow searchers to drill down farther. Despite your best efforts, an excellent advanced search will typically return hundreds or even thousands of websites. The average web searcher will only look at the first ten or twenty returns, hoping the information needed is found quickly.

Table 10-2. Image of Yahoo! Basic Search Page

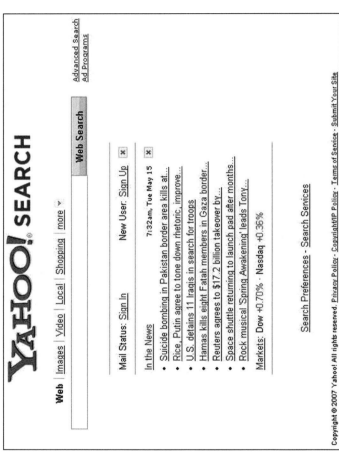

Table 10-3. Yahoo! Basic Search Results

YAHOO! SEARCH

Web | Images | Video | Local | Shopping | **more »**

"unauthorized practice of law"   Search   Advanced Search

Search Results   1 - 10 of about 191,000

◉ Also try: **unauthorized practice of law** attorney   More...

1. Practice of law - Wikipedia, the free encyclopedia
   Most **unauthorized practice of law** may be unintentional. ... See generally Jonathan Rose,
   "**Unauthorized Practice** of Law in Arizona: A Legal and Political ....
   en.wikipedia.org/wiki/Practice_of_law - 21k - Cached - More from this site

2. Virginia State Bar - Professional Regulation - **Unauthorized Practice of Law**
   ... Statement of the VSB's Standing Committee on **Unauthorized Practice of Law** ... opinions
   explaining what activities constitute the **unauthorized practice of law**. ...
   www.vsb.org/site/regulation/unauthorized-practice - 20k - Cached - More from this site

3. **Unauthorized practice of law**
   CAN YOU BE CHARGED WITH THE **UNAUTHORIZED PRACTICE OF LAW**? ... Liability for the
   unauthorized practice of law can be avoided by: ...
   www.kaarmls.com/unauthorizedpractice.htm - 40k - Cached - More from this site

4. Board on the **Unauthorized Practice of Law**
   The Board on the **Unauthorized Practice of Law** of the Supreme Court of ... to the Supreme
   Court in cases involving the alleged **unauthorized practice of law**. ...
   www.sconet.state.oh.us/UPL - 38k - Cached - More from this site

Reproduced with permission of Yahoo! Inc. YAHOO! and the YAHOO! logo are trademarks of Yahoo! Inc.

Table 10-4. Image of Yahoo! Advanced Search Page

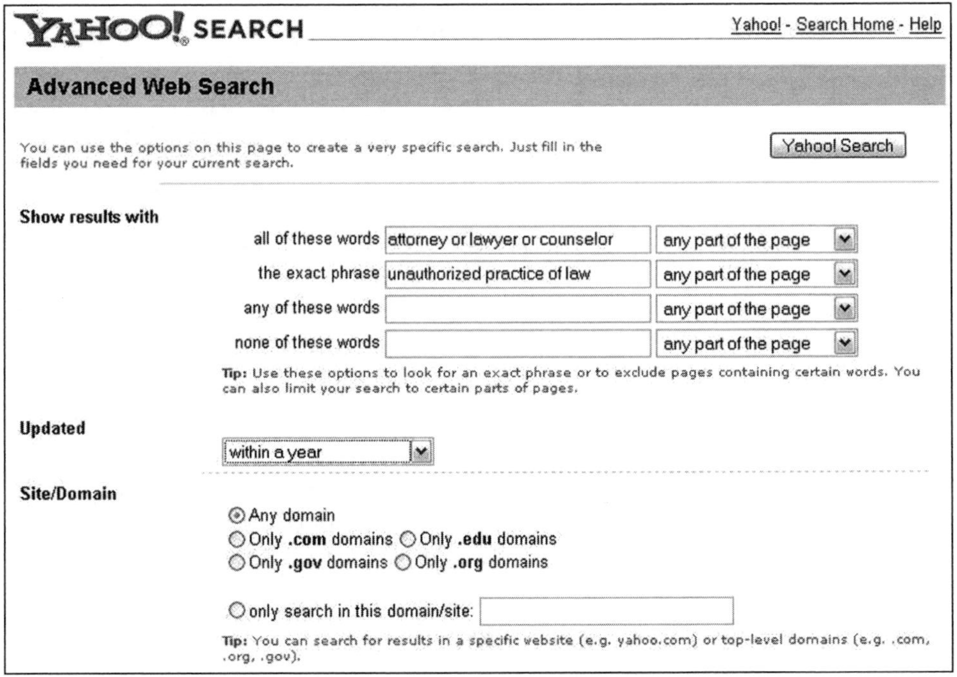

Reproduced with permission of Yahoo! Inc. YAHOO! and the YAHOO! logo are trademarks of Yahoo! Inc.

Table 10-5. Image of Yahoo! Advanced Search Results

YAHOO! SEARCH

Web | Images | Video | Local | Shopping | more »   Search   Advanced Search

attorney or lawyer or counselor "unauthorized practice of la
within a year

1 - 10 of about 1,620 for atto

Search Results

1. **Attorney** at law - Wikipedia, the free encyclopedia
... **attorney**-at-law and **attorney** and **counselor** (or ... law by an "out-of-state" **lawyer** is considered the **unauthorized practice of law** within that state. ...
en.wikipedia.org/wiki/Attorney - 57k - Cached - More from this site

2. MyAZBar::: **Unauthorized Practice of Law**
Using the designations "**lawyer**," "**attorney** at law," **counselor** at law," "law", ... to be engaging in the **unauthorized practice of law** or the Bar may refer, coordinate, ...
www.myazbar.org/LawyerRegulation/upl.cfm - 43k - Cached - More from this site

3. Avoiding the Unauthorized Practice of (PDF)
... and ensure that such non-**lawyer** assistants do not engage in the **unauthorized practice** ... **attorney**, constitute the **unauthorized practice of law**. 18 ...
milehighala.org/sem/Winter2004/pdf/Kueck_article_final_edit0803.pdf - 171k - View as html - More from this site

4. **UNAUTHORIZED PRACTICE OF LAW** BY LOCALLY IN-HOUSE COUNSEL (PDF)
... **attorney**-at-law, (6) assume, use or advertise the title of **lawyer**, **attorney** and ... **at-law**, **counselor-at-law**, **attorney**, **counselor**, **attorney** and **counselor**, or an ...
www.ethicsandlawyering.com/Issues/files/ConnUPL.pdf - 36k - View as html - More from this site

Table 10-6. Selected Search Techniques:
LexisNexis and Westlaw Compared

Search Technique	LexisNexis	Westlaw
and	and	&
or	or	a space between two words
and not -or- but not	and not	%
within same sentence	w/s	/s
within same paragraph	w/p	/p
Natural Language Searching	allows you to ask a research question in plain English	allows you to ask a research question in plain English
Easy Search	allows you to enter search terms without guidelines imposed by terms and connector or natural language searching	N/A
Terms and Connectors searching	search technique that employs the use of Boolean operators (such as "and," "or," "not") and segments	search technique that employs the use of Boolean operators (such as "and," "or," "not") and fields
root expander	!	!

Similar to basic and advanced search techniques on search engines, commercial vendors employ Natural Language (basic) and Terms and Connectors (advanced) searches. In addition, both search engines and commercial vendors have developed specialized techniques such as field or segment searching to foster efficient searching. Use vendor-supplied help screens and search templates as your guide. Table 10-6 provides a comparison of selected search techniques on Lexis-Nexis and Westlaw. Search techniques are also offered in each chapter of this book when relevant to the sources being discussed.

V. Online Search Help

Each vendor typically provides online help screens. In addition, most provide templates with suggested search terms, connectors, and lists of searchable fields or segments. In addition to these self-help features, most vendors also offer free consultations by telephone, on-line chat, or webinar. Phone numbers and links to the online chat feature are prominently displayed on vendor websites. You are encouraged to seek their advice when selecting databases and planning searches.

Chapter 11

Research Strategies and Organization

After reading this chapter you will be able to:

- determine whether to start your research with primary or secondary sources;
- keep a record of your research strategy;
- organize your research;
- take effective notes;
- determine when to update your sources in the research process;
- outline your legal analysis; and
- determine when to stop your research.

I. Moving from Story to Strategy

In practice, a client will come to your office with a problem and ask for help in solving it. The client will focus on facts that are important to him, without regard to whether they are legally significant. The client may have a desired solution in mind; that solution may best be obtained through legal remedies, or through mediation, family counseling, management strategies, or other means.

Your job will be to sift through the client's story to identify the legal issues. This may include asking questions to probe for facts the client may not immediately remember but which may have important legal consequences. Your job may also include reviewing documents such as contracts, letters, bills, or public records. In addition, you may need to interview other people who are involved in the client's situation.

Sometimes you will not be able to identify the legal issues immediately. Especially in an unfamiliar area of law, you may need to do some initial research to learn about the legal issues that affect the client's situation. Once you have some background in the relevant law, you should determine which legal issues affect the client's situation and begin to formulate a comprehensive research strategy.

II. Planning Your Research Strategy

The research process presented in Chapter 1 contains eight steps: (1) generate a list of *research terms*; (2) determine whether the issue is controlled by *state law*, *federal law*, or *both*; (3) consult *secondary sources* and practice aids, including treatises, legal encyclopedias, *American Law Reports*, and law review articles; (4) find controlling *constitutional provisions*, *statutes*, or *rules*; (5) use *online tools* or *digests* to find citations to cases; (6) read the cases either online or in *reporters*; (7) *update* by using a citator to ensure your legal authorities have not been repealed, reversed, modified, or otherwise changed; and (8) *outline* your legal analysis based on your research.

How you begin depends on the project. When researching an unfamiliar area of law, you will probably be more successful if you begin with secondary sources. In contrast, if you are familiar with an area of statutory law from previous work, your research may be more effective if you go directly to an annotated code. As a third example, if you work for an attorney who gives you a citation to a case she knows is relevant, you may want to begin by updating the case or using its topics and key numbers in a West digest. Both steps may quickly provide more cases on point. Finally, if your supervisor knows that the issue is controlled by common law, you may feel comfortable not researching statutory or constitutional provisions, or spending very little time in those areas.

The research process is not necessarily linear. Research terms are useful in searching the print indexes or online databases of secondary sources and statutes, as well as digests. Secondary sources may cite relevant statutes or cases. Updating may reveal more cases that you need to read, or it may uncover a new law review article that is on

Table 11-1. The Recursive Process of Research

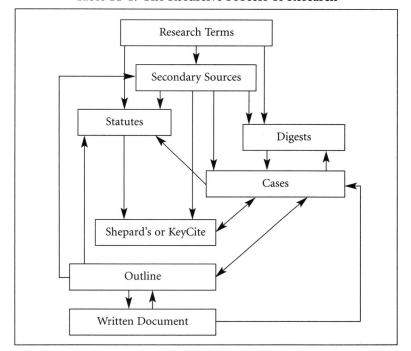

point. As you learn more about a project, you may want to review whether your earlier research was effective. Even as you begin writing, you may need to do more research if new issues arise or if you need more support for an argument. The flow chart in Table 11-1 gives an idea of how this process works.[1]

III. Taking Notes

Take careful notes throughout the research process. Taking notes can help you avoid duplicating steps, especially if you have to inter-

---

1. To simplify an already complicated flow chart, constitutional provisions, administrative law, and legislative history are omitted.

rupt your research for a notable length of time. Analytical notes also provide a basis for organizing and writing your document. These notes do not have to be formal or typed; in fact, you might waste valuable time by following too much structure or stopping to type your notes.

Do not underestimate the learning process that occurs while taking notes. Deciding what is important enough to include in notes and expressing those ideas in your own words will increase your understanding of the legal issues involved. Printing pages and highlighting sections of them do not provide this same analytical advantage.

IV. Organizing Your Research

Keeping your research organized is a means to efficient research, not an end in itself. The only "right" way to organize your research is the way that best helps you perform effective research, understand the legal issues, and analyze the problem. The following method will work for taking notes either on a laptop or on a legal pad. For researchers working with paper and pen, "create a document" simply means turning to a new page in your legal pad. Consider using color-coded sticky notes to tab each new document so that you do not get lost in a sea of paper. Some researchers prefer to keep notes of primary authorities on index cards rather than on sheets of paper or in computer files. If so, you will need some sort of box or a combination of clips and rubber bands to keep the cards organized.

Regardless of whether you take notes on your computer or on paper, you will need a three-ring binder or a set of files in which you keep hard copies of the most important authorities. If you decide to keep electronic files, you must create a similar file system by creating folders. Remember to back up your work often. Electronic files can easily become corrupt or disappear.

Tab the binder—or label the electronic files or folders—with the following headings: strategy/process, secondary sources, list of primary authorities, statutes (include rules and constitutional provisions here), cases, updating, and outline. Keep organization in perspective.

Spending extra time tabbing documents may make you more efficient, or it may be a form of procrastination.

A. Strategy and Process Trail

The first document you create should be your research *strategy*. This is simply a list of the different types of legal resources you intend to search. Writing out your strategy will help you ensure that you check all relevant sources of law. It may also make a new project seem less overwhelming, since the strategy will contain definite steps. You should refer to this document frequently to be sure you are keeping on track. In developing your strategy, remember to ask yourself the following questions:

- Is this issue controlled by state law, federal law, or both?
- Are there statutes or constitutional provisions on point or is this an area left to common law?
- Are administrative rules or decisions likely to be involved?
- Where in the research process will online sources be more effective and cost efficient than print sources?
- What period of time needs to be researched?
- How long do I have to complete the project?

Feel free to revise your strategy as you learn more about the issues. For instance, you may read a case with a related cause of action that you had not considered or you may encounter an article that highlights a relevant federal claim. If so, you need to adjust your research accordingly.

Your strategy should include a list of research terms that you generate from the facts and issues of your research problem. Brainstorm broadly to develop an expansive list. Refer to this list as you begin work in each new resource. Note on the list which terms were helpful in which resource. Add new terms to the list as you discover them. This list is especially likely to grow during your initial efforts if you begin with a secondary source that provides context for the research project.

Next, begin a *process trail*. While the strategy document outlines what you intend to do in your research, the process trail records what you actually did. By comparing the two, you will stay on track in your research and avoid duplicating work. Some researchers keep copious notes on their strategy document, so that in essence it becomes the process trail. With experience, you will develop a system that is comfortable and efficient for you.

As you begin with a new resource, make notes in your process trail that summarize your work in that resource. For print research, include the volumes you used, the indexes or tables you reviewed, and the terms you searched for. For computer research, include the website, the specific database or link, and the searches that you entered. List both successful and unsuccessful index terms and searches so that you do not inadvertently repeat these same steps later, or so you can revisit a "dead end" that later becomes relevant. Note the date that you performed each search.

LexisNexis and Westlaw provide an additional way to document your process trail for online research. In LexisNexis, use the "History" link at the top of the page to view your searches from the last 24 hours under the "Recent Results" tab. In addition, you can view your searches from the last 30 days by clicking on the "Archived Activity" tab. Although archived searches are deleted 30 days after your original search, you can preserve a particular LexisNexis search for longer than 30 days by clicking on the "Re-run/Edit" link to run it again. It will be added under your "Recent Results" tab and moved to your "Archived Activity" after 24 hours. Table 11-2 provides an image of the LexisNexis History service.

In Westlaw, click on the "Research Trail" link and then the "List of All Research Trails" link to access your searches run during the past 14 days. As you approach the expiration date, you can reset your research trail to expire in an additional 14 days by clicking on the "Reset" link provided. An image of Westlaw's Research Trail menu is provided in Table 11-3. Clicking on a specific Research Event listed on the Research Trail menu allows you to view the details of that Research Event, as exemplified by the image in Table 11-4.

The History service on LexisNexis and the Research Trail service on Westlaw are wonderful tools. However, you must be diligent about resetting or rerunning your searches so that they will not expire. Alternatively, you can print your searches so that you have a record of them.

Table 11-2. Image of the LexisNexis History Service

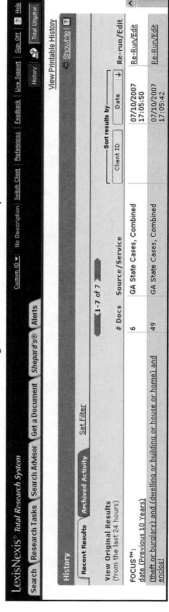

Copyright 2006 LexisNexis, a division of Reed Elsevier Inc. All Rights reserved. LexisNexis and the Knowledge Burst logo are registered trademarks of Reed Elsevier Properties Inc. and are used with the permission of LexisNexis.

Table 11-3. Image of Westlaw's Research Trail Menu

Westlaw.   FIND&PRINT   KEYCITE   DIRECTORY   KEYSEARCH   COURT DOCS   SITE MAP   HELP   SIGN OFF
                                                                              Preferences   Alert Center   Research Trail

Law School | Westlaw | New York | Legislative History-State | Legislative History – Fed | Add/Remove Tabs

Research Trail   Current Research Trail | New Research Trail

List of All Research Trails

Research Trail			Client ID	Date Last Accessed▾	Expiration (Days)		Notes
07/10/2007 03:46PM	Rename	Delete	AD	07/10/2007 03:46 PM	14	Reset	Add Note
07/05/2007 04:04PM	Rename	Delete	AD	07/05/2007 04:56 PM	9	Reset	Add Note
07/03/2007 02:32PM	Rename	Delete	AD	07/03/2007 04:02 PM	7	Reset	Add Note
07/03/2007 02:01PM	Rename	Delete	AD	07/03/2007 02:24 PM	7	Reset	Add Note
07/02/2007 03:45PM	Rename	Delete	AD	07/02/2007 04:00 PM	6	Reset	Add Note
06/27/2007 12:16PM	Rename	Delete	AD	06/27/2007 03:00 PM	1	Reset	Add Note
06/27/2007 11:58AM	Rename	Delete	AD	06/27/2007 12:13 PM	1	Reset	Add Note
06/26/2007 12:12PM	Rename	Delete	AD	06/26/2007 12:34 PM	0	Reset	Add Note

Reprinted from Westlaw with permission of Thomson/West.

Table 11-4. Image of Westlaw's Detailed Research Trail

Reprinted from Westlaw with permission of Thomson/West.

B. Secondary Authorities

Write a one-page summary for each secondary source you consult. Begin your summary with the title, author, and other citation information for the source. In your own words, summarize the relevant analysis in the source, including references to specific pages. Try to include a few sentences of how this source relates to your research. Does it explain the background of a statute? Does it trace the development of a line of cases? Does it criticize the law in your jurisdiction? Does it suggest a novel approach to your problem? Additionally, note any references to primary authorities that may be on point, and include these in your list of primary authorities.

The goals of reading secondary sources are usually to obtain an overview of an area of law and to locate citations to primary authority. These goals can be met by referring to secondary sources in books in the library or by skimming them online, without the waste of printing out numerous pages of text. Moreover, many law review articles may initially seem helpful but you may discover that they concentrate on a narrow point that is not applicable to your situation.

C. List of Primary Authorities

Create a list of primary sources that will contain the name and citation for all the primary authorities that you need to read. Throughout your research, as you come across a potentially relevant authority, include it on your list. This will allow you to maintain your train of thought with one resource while ensuring that you keep track of important cites to check later. After creating a list that includes a number of sources, check for duplicates before reading the authorities.

D. Analytical Notes on Primary Authority

At frequent points, stop and read the primary authority that you are finding. Legal analysis occurs throughout the process of researching a legal issue; reading as you research will ensure that you are finding relevant material. Note that there are two different modes of reading while you research: fast skimming to determine whether a source is even relevant and slow, methodical reading to understand a relevant authority thoroughly.

Skim each authority first to decide whether it is relevant. This is one of the most time-consuming activities for a novice researcher, but the following suggestions may help. For statutes and rules, skim through sections that provide definitions or explain the purpose. Focus on operative language that sets out duties or proscribes certain conduct. Quickly glance at provisions codified just before or after your provision to see whether they are relevant. For cases, begin by reading the synopsis at the beginning of the case. Then skim the headnotes to find the portion of the case that is possibly on point. Go directly to that portion of the case and read it. This probably means skipping over the procedural history, the facts of the case, and analysis of unrelated points of law.

If the source contains relevant material, make a few notes on your list of authorities. If it is not relevant, strike through it on your list. On your computer, use the "reviewing" or "commenting" toolbar to strike through these authorities. Do not completely delete or erase irrelevant authorities; otherwise, you may later find yourself accidentally reading them again.

Once you have selected a number of relevant authorities, choose an organizational scheme for reading them carefully in groups. If there is a constitutional provision, statute, or rule on point, begin by reading it carefully, then move to reading cases that interpret the provision. One approach is to read cases in chronological order, so that you see the development of the law over time. This may be time-consuming for causes of action that have existed for many years. Except for historical research, impose an artificial cut-off of twenty or thirty years in the past, so that you put your effort into recent law. The opposite approach works in many situations: by beginning with the recent cases, you avoid spending time learning old law that has been revised or superseded.

On this second, slower reading of relevant authorities, pay attention to parts that you may have skipped earlier while skimming. Read carefully the definitions in statutes. Be sure you understand the procedural posture of each case, since this affects the standard of review applied. Also be sure that you understand the facts of cases. Drawing a timeline or a chart of the relationships between the parties may be helpful. As you read through the case, cross out portions dealing with legal issues that are not confronting your client. If you decide that the case is actually not important, mark that on the first page so that you will not waste time reading it again.

When researching several issues or related claims, consider them one at a time. In this instance, you may have several lists of primary authorities, one for each claim you are researching. You may want to create a different binder or set of folders for each claim.

1. Notes on Statutes

Your notes should include both the actual statutory language and your outline of it. Because the exact words of statutes are so important, you should print, photocopy, or electronically save the text of these provisions.

To fully understand a complex statute, you should outline it. Highlighting is sufficient only if the statute is very short and clear. The statute may provide the elements of the claim or may control the period in which a claim can be brought. Outlining each statute will help you understand it better. Consult Table 4-3 for an example of an outlined statute.

Be sure to refer to the definition sections of statutes; where important terms are not defined, make a note to look for judicial definitions. Also be sure to read statutes that are cross-referenced in any pertinent statute.

2. Notes on Cases

When you decide that a case is relevant, you should brief it. The brief does not have to follow any formal style. Instead, the brief for each case should be a set of notes that highlight the key aspects of the case that are relevant for your research problem. Create a short summary of the pertinent facts, holding, and reasoning. You may choose to do this on your computer, creating a document or a page of a document for each case. You might prefer to write your summary in your legal pad or create an index card. Each case brief should include the following information:

Citation. Including the full citation will make writing the document easier because you avoid referring back to the original.

Facts. Include only those facts that are relevant to your project.

Holding and reasoning. Summarize the court's analysis, focusing on the holding and the reasoning that supports it. (Remember that the holding is the answer to the legal question raised by the case.) The holding is best expressed as a sentence that includes the legal issue, key facts, and rationale. As noted in Chapter 2, address only those issues in the case that are relevant to your project. For example, if a case includes both a tort claim and a related contract claim, but the contract claim is not relevant to your project, there is no need for you to thoroughly understand and take notes on the contract claim. Skim that section to be sure there is no relevant information hidden there, then ignore it.

Pinpoint pages. For case information that you will cite in your written document, include the pinpoint cite. Be sure that the pinpoint is to the authority you have been asked to cite in your document, not a parallel cite. This is especially important when printing online documents in which pagination in different reporters is indicated solely by an asterisk or two.

Reflections. Include your thoughts on the case. How do you anticipate using this case in your analysis? Does it resolve certain issues for your problem? Does it raise new questions?

Updating information. Each case brief should have a designated space for updating. Whether you use Shepard's or KeyCite, you must update each case that you use in your analysis.

E. Updating

You will likely find yourself updating at several points during the research process. Updating with Shepard's or KeyCite early in the process will lead you to other authorities on point. Updating before you begin to rely on an authority is critical; you must verify that each authority you include in your analysis is still "good law." Updating just before submitting a document ensures that nothing has changed while you were working on the project.

As you update each authority, make notes on your case briefs and statute outlines as to when you updated authorities, whether the authorities are still respected, and what new sources you found. Recording the date of your updating search will be helpful when you perform your final update just before submitting your document. You will only have to check citing sources that became available since your last update.

Printing lists of citations is an easy and efficient way to compare new citations with your list of primary authorities. Keep these lists in the *updating* section of your binder.

F. Outlining Your Analysis

Because the most effective research often occurs in conjunction with the analysis of your particular project, try to develop an outline that addresses your client's problem as soon as you can. The visual learner may benefit from a chart that organizes all the primary authority by issue or element, such as in Table 11-5, following the typical legal analysis format of Issue-Rule-Application-Conclusion (IRAC).

Table 11-5 shows the initial stages of legal analysis when the research is determining whether each case is relevant to the project. Remember that thorough legal analysis will require you to synthesize a rule from the relevant statute and cases and then apply that rule to the facts of your client's case. Refer to the texts listed in Appendix B for further guidance on legal analysis.

Your first analytical outline or chart may be based on information in a secondary source, the requirements of a statute, or the elements of a common law claim. It will become more sophisticated and detailed as you conduct your research. Recognize that you cannot reread

Table 11-5. Sample Analysis Chart

Research Question: Has a person committed the crime of burglary if she enters the frame of a newly constructed home with the intent to steal building supplies?

Controlling Statute: O.C.G.A. § 16-7-1(a) (2006)

"A person commits the offense of burglary when, without authority and with the intent to commit a felony or theft therein, he enters or remains within the dwelling house of another or any building, vehicle, railroad car, watercraft, or other such structure designed for use as the dwelling of another...."

Issue	Cases	Rule	Application	Conclusion
Whether the frame of a home that has never been occupied is considered a "dwelling" or a "building."	*Smith v. State,* 226 Ga. App. 9, 11–12 (1997)	"A building includes a house under construction which is so far completed as to be capable of providing shelter to people, animals, or property...."	House under construction, but frame not capable of providing shelter.	Because house cannot yet provide shelter, it is not a dwelling.
	Redfern v. State, 246 Ga. App. 572, 575 (2000)	For broadcast tower, element of enclosure for people, animals, or goods is lacking.	Not enclosed yet.	Unenclosed, so not a dwelling.
	Garrett v. State, 259 Ga. App. 870, 871 (2002)	To determine whether it is a building the purpose of the structure should be considered.	Not enclosed yet, but purpose is to shelter people after construction is complete.	Since the purpose is for the structure to be enclosed and shelter people, it can be considered a dwelling.

every case or statute in its entirety each time you need to include it in your outline; instead, refer to your notes and briefs to find the key ideas supporting each step in your analysis.

The outline or chart should enable you to synthesize the law, apply the law to your client's facts, and reach a conclusion on the desired outcome. Applying the law to your client's facts may lead you to research issues that may not be apparent in a merely theoretical discussion of the law.

G. Ending Your Research

One of the most difficult problems new researchers face is deciding when to stop researching and begin writing. Often deadlines imposed by the court or a supervisor will limit the amount of time spent on a research project. The expense to the client will also be a consideration.

Apart from these practical constraints, most legal researchers want to believe that if they search long enough they will find a case or statute or article or *something* that answers the client's legal question clearly and definitively. Sometimes that happens; if you find the answer, you know your research is over. Even without finding a clear answer, when your research in various sources leads back to the same authorities, you can be confident that you have been thorough. As a final checklist, go through each step of the basic research process to ensure you considered each one. Then review your strategy and process trail for this particular project.

If you have worked through the research process and found nothing, it may be that nothing exists. Before reaching that conclusion, expand your research terms and look in a few more secondary sources. Consider whether other jurisdictions may have helpful persuasive authority.

Remember that the goal of your research is to solve a client's problem. Sometimes the law will not seem to support the solution that your client had in mind. Think creatively to address the client's problem in a different way. While you must tell your supervisor or your client when a desired approach is not feasible, you will want to have prepared an alternate solution if possible.

Appendix A

Legal Citation

To convince another lawyer or a judge that you thoroughly researched your argument and that your ideas are well supported, you must provide references to the authorities you used to develop your analysis and reach your conclusion. These references are called *legal citations*. They tell the reader where to find the authorities you rely on and indicate the level of analytical support the authorities provide.[1] In a legal document, every legal rule and every explanation of the law must be cited. The purposes of legal citations are listed in Table A-1.

Table A-1. Purposes of Legal Citations

1. Show the reader where to find the cited material in the original case, statute, rule, article, or other authority.

2. Indicate the weight and persuasiveness of each authority, for example, by specifying the court that decided the case, the author of a document, and the publication date of the authority.

3. Convey the type and degree of support the authority offers, for example, by indicating whether the authority supports your point directly or only implicitly.

4. Demonstrate that the analysis in your document is well researched and well supported.

5. Give credit to those who originated an idea you are presenting.

Source: *ALWD Citation Manual.*

---

1. Association of Legal Writing Directors & Darby Dickerson, *ALWD Citation Manual: A Professional System of Citation* 3 (3d ed. 2006).

Legal citations are included in the text of legal documents rather than being saved for a bibliography. While law students initially feel that these citations clutter documents, lawyers appreciate the valuable information that they provide.

The format used to convey citation information requires meticulous attention to such riveting details as whether a space is needed between two abbreviations. In this respect, citation format rules can be like fundamental writing rules, which are based on convention, not reason. Why capitalize the personal pronoun "I" but not "we" or "you" or "they"? Why does a comma signify a pause, while a period indicates a stop? Rather than trying to understand why citations are formatted the way they are, the most practical approach is simply to learn citation rules and apply them. Frequent repetition will make them second nature.

Of the many different citation systems that exist, this chapter addresses Georgia citation rules as well as the two national citation manuals, the *ALWD Citation Manual: A Professional System of Citation* (hereinafter *ALWD Manual*)[2] and *The Bluebook: A Uniform System of Citation* (hereinafter *Bluebook*).[3] In law practice, you may encounter state statutes, court rules, and style manuals that dictate the form of citation used before the courts of different states. You may find that each firm or agency that you work for has its own preference for citation or makes minor variations to generally accepted formats. Some law offices have their own style manuals, drawn from state rules and national manuals. Once you learn what your employer's preferences are, adjust your citation format accordingly. Similarly, in law school, learn the style of the teacher you are working with or the journal you are a member of. Once you are aware of the basic function and format of citation, adapting to a slightly different set of rules will not be difficult.

Most states have their own rules of citation, called *local rules.* These rules differ somewhat from the rules of other states and the rules in the two national citation manuals. The national citation manuals recognize this fact and include information about local rules. In

---

2. *Id.*

3. *The Bluebook: A Uniform System of Citation* (Columbia Law Review et al. eds., 18th ed. 2005).

the *Bluebook* you will find citations to the local rules in Table BT.2, "Jurisdiction-Specific Citation Rules and Style Guides." The *ALWD Manual* contains the text of court rules in Appendix 2, "Local Court Citation Rules." Another excellent source for local rules of citation is Peter Martin's Table of State-Specific Citation Norms and Practices in *Introduction to Basic Legal Citation (LII 2006 ed.)*, which is available at www.law.cornell.edu/citation/7-500.htm.

I. Georgia Citation Rules

In Georgia, there are two sources of local rules that address citation style. The first can be found in the statutes. According to O.C.G.A. § 1-1-8(e), the "Official Code of Georgia Annotated published under authority of the State of Georgia may be cited or referred to as 'O.C.G.A.'"[4] This differs from both the *Bluebook* and the *ALWD Manual*, which use the abbreviation "Ga. Code Ann." You will see the abbreviation "Ga. Code Ann." in cases and secondary source materials from other jurisdictions.

The second source of local rules is the court. According to Supreme Court and Court of Appeals rules, citations to Georgia cases should include the volume and page number of the official reporter (*Georgia Reports* and *Georgia Appeals Reports*).[5] Citations to cases not reported should include the Supreme Court or Court of Appeals case number and the date of the decision. For further citation guidance, you can use either the *Bluebook* or the *ALWD Manual* for Georgia citations. Table A-2 provides examples of Georgia citations using local rules and *Bluebook* practitioner rules.

The federal courts in Georgia also have local citation rules. The local rules for the U.S. Court of Appeals for the Eleventh Circuit give attorneys the choice of using the *Bluebook* or the *ALWD Manual*.[6] The local rules for the U.S. District Court for the Northern District of

---

4. O.C.G.A. § 1-1-8(e) (2000).
5. Ga. Sup. Ct. R. 22; Ga. Ct. App. R. 24(d).
6. 11th Cir. R. 28-1(k).

Table A-2. Example Citations to Georgia Primary Sources

Constitution	Ga. Const. art. VI, §6, para. 3	
Statutes	Text in main volume	O.C.G.A. §2-14-130 (2000)
	Text in pocket part	O.C.G.A. §10-1-393.6 (Supp. 2006)
Session Laws	1996 Ga. Laws 453	
Reported Cases	*Clark v. State*, 271 Ga. 6, 515 S.E.2d 155 (1999) *Johnson v. Brueckner*, 216 Ga. App. 52, 453 S.E.2d 76 (1994)	
Unreported Cases	*Nelson v. Haugabrook*, No. A06A1137 (Ga. App. Nov. 15, 2006)	
Regulations	Ga. Comp. R. & Regs. r. 300-8-1 (1983)	
Court Rules	Ga. Sup. Ct. R. 24	

Georgia address citation to federal statutes and regulations but do not mention case citations.[7]

The only published citation guide for Georgia legal materials is Appendix V of *Guide to Georgia Legal Research and Legal History* by Leah F. Chanin and Suzanne L. Cassidy. The citation guide primarily follows the *Bluebook* but includes detailed information about historical cases, constitutions, and statutes. It also includes citation examples for secondary materials and ethics and state bar rules. A summary of abbreviations for Georgia material appears in Table 1 of the *Bluebook* (page 206) and Appendix 1 of the *ALWD Manual* (pages 368–69).

II. The National Citation Manuals

While local citation rules often provide only rules and examples, national citation manuals attempt to explain the components of ci-

---

7. N.D. Ga. R. 5.1(F).

tations. Student editors of four Ivy League law reviews have developed citation rules that are published as the *Bluebook*, now in its eighteenth edition. An author submitting an article for publication in one of those law reviews, or in other law reviews that adhere to *Bluebook* rules, should follow *Bluebook* citation format. The *Bluebook* was first published in 1926 and remains the standard for legal citations. Many lawyers refer to the process of checking cites in a legal document as "bluebooking." However, the *Bluebook* has two citation systems — one for law review articles and another for legal memoranda and court documents. The two systems can be confusing for novices. The *ALWD Manual*, first published in 2000, may be a better choice for novices because it uses a single system of citation for legal memoranda, court documents, law review articles, and all other legal documents. The explanations are clear, and the examples are useful to both law students and practicing attorneys.

A. Incorporating Citations into a Document

You must provide a citation for each idea that comes from a case, statute, article, or other source. Thus, paragraphs that state legal rules and explain the law should contain many citations. A citation may offer support for an entire sentence or for an idea expressed in part of a sentence. If the citation supports the entire sentence, it is placed in a separate *citation sentence* that begins with a capital letter and ends with a period. If the citation supports only a portion of the sentence, it is included immediately after the relevant part of that sentence and set off from the sentence by commas in what is called a *citation clause*. Table A-3 provides examples of each.

Do not cite your client's facts or your conclusions about a case, statute, or other authority. The following sentence should not be cited: "Under the facts presented, our client's conduct would fall under second-degree arson, since the fire occurred in an unoccupied vehicle." These facts and conclusions are unique to your situation and would not be found anywhere in the reference source.

Table A-3. Examples of Citation Sentences and Citation Clauses

Citation Sentences	A person commits arson by means of fire or explosive. O.C.G.A. § 16-7-60 (2003). The punishment for first degree arson is "a fine of not more than $50,000.00 or … imprisonment for not less than one nor more than 20 years, or both." O.C.G.A. § 16-7-60(c) (Supp. 2006).
Citation Clauses	Georgia statutes define both first-degree arson, O.C.G.A. § 16-7-60 (2003), and second-degree arson, O.C.G.A. § 16-7-61 (2003).

B. Case Citations

A full citation to a case includes (1) the name of the case, (2) the volume and reporter in which the case is published, (3) the first page of the case, (4) the exact page in the case that contains the idea you are citing (i.e., the *pinpoint* or *jump* cite), (5) the court that decided the case, (6) the date the case was decided, and (7) the subsequent history of the case, if any. The key points for citation to cases are given below, along with examples.

case name	volume, reporter, first page & pinpoint	court & year	subsequent history
Collier v. Marsh,	416 S.E.2d 849, 851	(Ga. Ct. App. 1992),	*overruled by Hobbs v. Arthur,* 434 S.E.2d 748 (Ga. Ct. App. 1993).

In the example above, the citation includes the regional reporter, *South Eastern Reporter, Second Series,* rather than the official reporter, *Georgia Appeals Reports.* If you are writing for the Georgia courts, you should use the official reporter as directed by the local rules discussed above. You can also include the parallel cite to *South Eastern Reporter.* However, if you are writing for any court other than the Georgia courts, you must include the regional reporter cite. This is because the regional reporters are more widely available than the official reporters. For example, a court in Texas will likely have access to the regional *South Eastern Reporter* and not *Georgia Reports* or *Georgia Appeals Reports*.

1. Essential Components of Case Citations

Include the name of just the first party on each side, even if several are listed in the case caption. If the party is an individual, include only the party's last name. If the party is a business or organization, shorten the party's name by using the abbreviations in *Bluebook* Table T.6 or *ALWD Manual* Appendix 3.

Between the parties' names, place a lower case "v" followed by a period. Do not use a capital "V" or use the abbreviation "vs." Place a comma after the second party's name; do not italicize this comma.

The parties' names may be italicized or underlined. Use the style preferred by your supervisor, and use that style consistently throughout each document. Do not combine italics and underlining in one cite or within a single document.

> EXAMPLE: *Harris v. Fla. Elections Comm'n*, 235 F.3d 578,
> 580 (11th Cir. 2000)

Next, give the volume and the reporter in which the case is found. Pay special attention to whether the reporter is in its first, second, or third series. Abbreviations for common reporters are found in Table T.1 of the *Bluebook* and on page 76 of the *ALWD Manual*. Georgia reporters are included on page 206 of the *Bluebook* and 368 of the *ALWD Manual*. In the example above, 235 is the volume number and F.3d is the reporter abbreviation for *Federal Reporter, Third Series*.

After the reporter name, include both the first page of the case and the pinpoint page containing the idea that you are referencing, separated by a comma and a space. The first page of the above case is 578, and the page where your idea came from is 580. If the pinpoint page you are citing is also the first page of the case, then the same page number will appear twice even though this seems repetitive. When using an online version of a case, remember that a reference to a specific reporter page may change in the middle of a computer screen or a printed page. This means that the page number indicated at the top of the screen or printed page may not correspond to the page where the relevant information is located in the original source. For example, if the notation *581 appeared in the text before the relevant information, the pinpoint cite would be to page 581, not page 580.

In a parenthetical following all of this information, indicate the court that decided the case, using abbreviations in Table T.1 of the *Bluebook* or Appendix 4 of the *ALWD Manual*. In both of the tables in the citation manuals, the court abbreviations are in parentheses after the name of each court. In the above example, the Eleventh Circuit Court of Appeals, a federal court, decided the case.

If the reporter abbreviation clearly indicates which court decided a case, do not repeat this information in the parenthetical. For example, only cases of the U.S. Supreme Court are reported in *United States Reports*, abbreviated U.S. Similarly, only cases decided by the Georgia Court of Appeals are reported in *Georgia Appeals Report*, abbreviated Ga. App. Thus, repeating court abbreviations in citations to those reporters would be duplicative. By contrast, *South Eastern Reporter, Second Series*, abbreviated S.E.2d, publishes decisions from different courts within several states, so the court that decided a particular case needs to be indicated parenthetically. Thus, in the last example below, "W. Va." indicates that the decision came from the West Virginia Supreme Court rather than from another court whose decisions are also published in this reporter.

EXAMPLES: *Brown v. Bd. of Educ.*, 349 U.S. 294 (1955)
Wells v. Beach, 169 Ga. App. 736 (1984)
Ray v. Mangum, 346 S.E.2d 52 (W. Va. 1986)

Note that these court abbreviations are not the same as postal codes. Abbreviating the West Virginia Supreme Court as WV would be incorrect.

The final piece of required information in most cites is the date the case was decided. For cases published in reporters, give only the year of decision, not the month or date. Do not confuse the date of decision with the date on which the case was argued or submitted, the date on which a motion for rehearing was denied, or the publication date of the reporter. For cases not published in a reporter you must provide the month, day, and year of the decision. See the example of an unreported case in Table A-2.

2. *Full and Short Citations to Cases*

The first time you mention a case by name, you must immediately give its full citation, including all of the information outlined above. Even though it is technically correct to include the full citation at the beginning of a sentence, a full citation takes up considerable space. By the time your reader gets through the citation and to your idea at the end of the sentence, the reader may have lost interest. The examples in Table A-4 illustrate this problem.

After a full citation has been used once to introduce an authority, short citations are subsequently used to cite this same authority. A short citation provides just enough information to allow the reader to locate the longer citation and find the pinpoint page.

When the immediately preceding cite is to the same source and the same page, use *id.* as the short cite. Note that the period after *id.* is italicized. When the second cite is to a different page within the same source, follow the *id.* with "at" and the new pinpoint page number. Capitalize *id.* when it begins a citation sentence, just as the beginning of any sentence is capitalized.

If the cite is to a source that has been fully cited already, but is not the immediately preceding cite, give the name of one of the parties (generally the first party named in the full cite), the volume, the reporter, and the pinpoint page following "at." For example, the case cited in Table A-4 may be cited as *Copher*, 220 Ga. App. at 44. The format, *Copher* at 44, consisting of just a case name and page number, is incorrect. The volume and reporter abbreviation are also needed.

3. *Prior and Subsequent History*

Sometimes your citation needs to show what happened to your case at an earlier or later stage of litigation. The case you are citing may have reversed an earlier case, as in the example below. If you are citing a case for a court's analysis of one issue and a later court

Table A-4. Examples of Full Citations

Assume that this is the first time the case has been mentioned in this
document.

CORRECT: Statutes are to be construed in connection and in
           harmony with existing law. *Copher v. Mackey*, 220
           Ga. App. 43, 44 (1996).

AVOID: In *Copher v. Mackey*, 220 Ga. App. 43, 44 (1996), the
           court noted that statutes are to be construed in con-
           nection and in harmony with existing law.

reversed only on the second issue, you need to alert your reader to
that reversal. Or, if you decide for historical purposes to include in
your document discussion of a case that was later overruled, your
reader needs to know that as soon as you introduce the case. Prior
and subsequent history can be appended to the full citations discussed above.

EXAMPLE: The only time that the Supreme Court ad-
           dressed the requirement of motive for an EM-
           TALA claim, the court rejected that require-
           ment. *Roberts v. Galen of Va.*, 525 U.S. 249, 253
           (1999), *rev'g* 111 F.3d 405 (6th Cir. 1997).

C. Federal Statutes

The general rule for citing federal laws is to cite the *United States
Code* (U.S.C.), which is the official code for federal statutes. In real-
ity, that publication is published so slowly that the current language
will most likely be found in a commercial code, either *United States
Code Annotated* (U.S.C.A.), published by West, or *United States Code
Service* (U.S.C.S.), published by LexisNexis.

A cite to a federal statute includes the title, code name, section,
publisher (except for U.S.C.), and date. The date given in statutory
cites is the date of the volume in which the statute is published, not
the date the statute was enacted. If the language of a portion of the

statute is reprinted in the pocket part, include the dates of both the bound volume and the pocket part. If the language appears only in the pocket part, include only the date of the pocket part.

> EXAMPLE: Statutory language appears in the bound vol-
> ume only:
> 28 U.S.C.A. § 1332 (West 2006)

> EXAMPLE: Statutory language appears in both the bound
> volume and the supplement:
> 49 U.S.C.A. § 5122 (West 1997 & Supp. 2006)

> EXAMPLE: Statutory language appears in just the supple-
> ment:
> 20 U.S.C.A. § 1409 (West Supp. 2006)

If you are using an online resource, include the name of the database and information regarding currency provided by the database itself rather than the year of the bound volume of the code books.

D. Signals

A citation must show the reader that you understand the level of support each authority provides. You do this by deciding whether to use an introductory signal and, if so, which one. The more common signals are explained in Table A-5.

E. Explanatory Parentheticals

At the end of a citation, you can append additional information about the authority in parentheses. Sometimes this parenthetical information conveys to the reader the weight of the authority. For example, a case may have been decided *en banc* or *per curiam*. Or the case may have been decided by a narrow split among the judges who heard the case. Parenthetical information also allows you to name the judges who joined in a dissenting, concurring, or plurality opinion. An explanatory parenthetical following a signal can convey helpful, additional information in a compressed space. When using this type

Table A-5. Common Signals

No signal	The source (i) directly states the proposition, (ii) identifies the source of a quotation, or (iii) identifies an authority referred to in the text.
See	The source clearly supports the proposition. "*See*" is used when the proposition is not directly stated by the cited authority but obviously follows from it; there is an inferential step between the authority cited and the proposition is supports.
See also	The source cited provides additional support for the proposition.
E.g.	Many authorities state the proposition, and you are citing only one or a few as examples. This signal allows you to cite just one source while letting the reader know that many other sources say the same thing.

Source: The *Bluebook*, Rule 1.2, p. 46.

of parenthetical, be sure that you do not inadvertently hide a critical part of the court's analysis at the end of a long citation, where a reader is likely to skip over it.

> EXAMPLE: Excluding relevant evidence during a sentencing hearing may deny the criminal defendant due process. *Green v. Georgia*, 442 U.S. 95, 97 (1979) (per curiam) (regarding the testimony of a co-defendant's confession in a rape and murder case).

F. Quotations

Quotations should be used only when the reader needs to see the text exactly as it appears in the original authority. Of all the audiences you write for, trial courts will probably be most receptive to longer quotations. For example, quoting the controlling statutory language can be extremely helpful. As another example, if a well-known case explains an analytical point in a particularly insightful way, a quotation may be warranted.

Excessive quotation has two drawbacks. First, quotations interrupt the flow of your writing when the style of the quoted language differs from your own. Second, excessive use of quotations may suggest to the reader that you do not fully comprehend the material; it is much easier to cut and paste together a document from pieces of various cases than to synthesize and explain a rule of law. Quotations should not be used simply because you cannot think of another way to express an idea.

When a quotation is needed, the words, punctuation, and capitalization within the quotation marks must appear *exactly* as they do in the original. Treat a quotation as a photocopy of the original text. Any alterations or omissions must be indicated. Include commas and periods inside quotation marks; place other punctuation outside the quotation marks unless it is included in the original text. Also, try to provide smooth transitions between your text and the quoted text.

If a quotation contains fifty or more words, it must be indented on both sides and have justified margins, and it should not include quotation marks. Use the word count feature on your word processing program to determine how many words are in a quotation. When you indent a quotation in this manner, put the citation at the very beginning of the line following the quotation, without indentation. Quotations are discussed in Rule 5 of the *Bluebook* and in Rule 47 of the *ALWD Manual*.

G. Noteworthy Details

Paying attention to the following details will enhance your reputation as a careful and conscientious lawyer.

1. Use proper ordinal abbreviations. The most confusing are 2d for "Second" and 3d for "Third" because they differ from the standard format. See the tables in the back of the *Bluebook* that indicate the proper ordinal abbreviations for reporters and other publications, or use the *ALWD Manual* Rule 4.3.

2. Do not insert a space between abbreviations of single capital letters. For example, there is no space in U.S. Ordinal numbers like 1st, 2d, and 3d are considered single capital letters for purposes of this rule. Thus, there is no space in S.E.2d or F.3d because 2d and 3d are considered single capital letters. Leave one space between elements of an abbreviation that are not single capital letters. For example, F. Supp. 2d has a space on each side of "Supp." It would be incorrect to write F.Supp.2d.

3. Remember that in citation sentences and clauses, you abbreviate case names using the abbreviations in Tables T.6 and T.10 of the *Bluebook* or Appendix 3 of the *ALWD Manual*. However, do not abbreviate when using the case name in a textual sentence. For example, although you would use *Harris v. Fla. Elections Comm'n* in a citation sentence, in a textual sentence you would write *Harris v. Florida Elections Commission*.

4. Do not use "*supra*" or "*infra*" to refer to a case that you have already cited or will cite later in the document. Instead, use the proper short citation form in either a citation clause or a citation sentence, as appropriate.

5. It is most common in legal documents to spell out numbers zero through ninety-nine and to use numerals for larger numbers. However, you should always spell out a number that is the first word of a sentence.

III. Editing Citations

To be sure that the citations in your document correctly reflect your research and support your analysis, you should include enough time in the writing and editing process to check citation accuracy. As you are writing the document, refer frequently to the local rules or to the citation guide required by your supervisor. After you have completely finished writing the text of the document, check the citations carefully again. Be sure that each citation is still accurate after all the writing revisions you have made. For example, moving a sentence might require you to change an *id.* to another form of short cite, or vice versa. In fact, some careful writers do not insert *id.* citations until they are completely finished writing and revising.

There are two citation programs you can use to check your citations: CheckCite (available at www.lexisnexis.com/shepards/checkcite/features.asp) and WestCheck (available at http://westcheck.com). CheckCite is produced by LexisNexis and uses the Shepard's service to check citations, and WestCheck uses Westlaw's KeyCite program to check cites. Both programs can be used to extract citations from your document and then run them in the online databases to check party names, reporter cites, dates, and quotations. You can also insure none of your cases has been negatively affected by subsequent cases or statutes.

Even if you use a citation program to check the substance of your citations, you should review each citation yourself to be certain that it supports your text and is in the correct format. The time invested in checking citations is well spent if it enables the person reading your document to quickly find the authorities you cite and to understand your analysis.

Appendix B

Selected Bibliography

Georgia Research

Leah F. Chanin & Suzanne L. Cassidy, *Guide to Georgia Legal Research and Legal History* (Harrison Co. 1990 & Supp. 1997).

Melvin B. Hill, *The Georgia State Constitution: A Reference Guide* (Greenwood Press 1994).

Nancy P. Johnson, Nancy J. Adams, & Elizabeth G. Adelman, *Researching Georgia Law (2006 Edition)*, 22 Ga. St. U. L. Rev. 381 (2005).

Nancy P. Johnson, Kreig Kitts & Ronald Wheeler, Georgia Practice Materials: A Selective Annotated Bibliography, in Frank F. Houdek, ed., *State Practice Materials: Annotated Bibliographies* (W.S. Hein, 2006).

Kristina L. Neidringhaus, Georgia Pre-Statehood Legal Research, in *Prestatehood Legal Materials: A Fifty-State Research Guide, Including New York City and the District of Columbia* (Michael Chiorazzi & Marguerite Most eds., 2006).

General Research (tending to focus on federal material)

J.D.S. Armstrong & Christopher A. Knott, *Where the Law Is: An Introduction to Advanced Legal Research* (2d ed., Thomson/West 2006).

Robert C. Berring & Elizabeth A. Edinger, *Finding the Law* (12th ed., Thomson/West 2005).

Morris L. Cohen & Kent C. Olson, *Legal Research in a Nutshell* (9th ed., Thomson/West 2007).

Stephen Elias & Susan Levinkind, *Legal Research: How to Find and Understand the Law* (13th ed., Nolo Press 2005).

Christina L. Kunz et al., *The Process of Legal Research* (6th ed., Aspen Publishers 2004).

Roy M. Mersky & Donald J. Dunn, *Fundamentals of Legal Research* (8th ed., Found. Press 2002). Companion volume: *Legal Research Illustrated.*

Kent C. Olson, *Legal Information: How to Find It, How to Use It* (Oryx Press 1999).

Amy E. Sloan, *Basic Legal Research: Tools and Strategies* (3d ed., Aspen Publishers 2006).

Specialized Research

Ken Kozlowski, *The Internet Guide for the Legal Researcher* (3d ed., Infosources Publ'g 2001).

Lee F. Peoples, *Legal Ethics: A Research Guide* (2d ed., W.S. Hein 2006).

William A. Raabe, Gerald E. Whittenburg, & Debra L. Sanders, *Federal Tax Research* (7th ed., Thomson/South-Western 2006).

Gail Levin Richmond, *Federal Tax Research Guide to Materials and Techniques* (7th ed., Found. Press 2007).

Specialized Legal Research (Penny A. Hazelton, ed., 2006 Supp. Aspen Publishers).

Texts on Legal Analysis

Charles R. Calleros, *Legal Method and Writing* (5th ed., Aspen Publishers 2006).

Linda H. Edwards, *Legal Writing: Process, Analysis, and Organization* (4th ed., Aspen Publishers 2006).

Linda H. Edwards, *Legal Writing and Analysis* (2d ed., Aspen Publishers 2007).

Pamela Lysaght & Bradley G. Clary, *Successful Legal Analysis and Writing: The Fundamentals* (2d ed., Thomson/West 2006).

Michael D. Murray & Christy Hallam DeSanctis, *Legal Research, Writing, and Analysis* (Foundation Press 2006).

Richard K. Neumann, Jr., *Legal Reasoning and Legal Writing: Structure, Strategy, and Style* (5th ed., Aspen Publishers 2005).

Laurel Currie Oates & Anne Enquist, *The Legal Writing Handbook: Analysis, Research, and Writing* (4th ed., Aspen Publishers 2006).

Diana V. Pratt, *Legal Writing: A Systematic Approach* (4th ed., Thomson/West 2004).

Mary Barnard Ray & Barbara J. Cox, *Beyond the Basics: A Text for Advanced Legal Writing* (2d ed., Thomson/West 2003).

David S. Romantz & Kathleen Elliott Vinson, *Legal Analysis: The Fundamental Skill* (Carolina Academic Press 1998).

Deborah A. Schmedemann & Christina L. Kunz, *Synthesis: Legal Reading, Reasoning, and Writing* (3d ed., Aspen Publishers 2007).

Helene S. Shapo, Marilyn R. Walter, & Elizabeth Fajans, *Writing and Analysis in the Law* (rev. 4th ed., Found. Press 2003).

Appendix C

Selected List of Georgia Practice Materials

The list below is an abbreviated version of the *Subject Bibliography of Georgia Practice Materials* found in the law review article Johnson, Adams and Adelman, "Researching Georgia Law (2006 Edition)," 22 Ga. St. U. L. Rev. 381 (2005). The titles included here are standard practice books that are updated regularly. Books that have not been updated within the past five years are not included.

Subject Headings:

Alternative Dispute Resolution
Collections
Contracts
Corporations
Criminal Law
Damages
Debtor and Creditor
Elder Law
Eminent Domain
Employment and Labor
Environmental Law
Evidence
Family and Juvenile Law
Forms
General

Insurance
Jury Instructions
Landlord-Tenant Law
Medical Malpractice
Motor Vehicle Law
Practice and Procedure
Probate and Administration of Estates
Products Liability
Real Property
Securities
Security Interests
Taxation
Torts and Personal Injury
Workers' Compensation
Wrongful Death

Alternative Dispute Resolution

H. Sol Clark & Fred S. Clark, Georgia Settlements Law and Strategies (2d ed. 1999 & Supp. 2006). Suwanee, Ga.: Harrison Co. (a division of Thomson/West). Available on Westlaw.

Douglas H. Yarn & Gregory Todd Jones, Alternative Dispute Resolution: Practice and Procedure in Georgia (3d ed. 2006). St. Paul, Minn.: Thomson/West. Available on Westlaw.

Collections

Stuart Finestone, Georgia Post-Judgment Collection with Forms (4th ed. 2002 & Supp. 2007). St. Paul, Minn.: Thomson/West. Available on Westlaw.

Daniel F. Hinkel, Georgia Construction Mechanics' and Materialmen's Liens with Forms (3d ed. 1998 & Supp. 2006). Norcross, Ga.: Harrison Co. (a division of Thomson/West). Available on Westlaw.

Lewis N. Jones, Georgia Legal Collections. (2000 & Supp. 2006). Suwanee, Ga.: Harrison Co. (a division of Thomson/West). Available on Westlaw.

Contracts

John K. Larkins, Jr., Georgia Contracts: Law and Litigation (2002 & Supp. 2007). Suwanee, Ga.: Harrison Co. (a division of Thomson/West). Available on Westlaw.

Corporations

David Jon Fischer, et al., Georgia Corporate Forms (2005 & Supp. 2006). 2 vols. San Francisco, CA: LexisNexis. Published biennially. Available on LexisNexis.

Jerome L. Kaplan, et al., Kaplan's Nadler Georgia Corporations, Limited Partnerships, and Limited Liability Companies with Forms (2007 ed.). 2 vols. St. Paul, Minn.:

Thomson/West. Published annually. Available on Westlaw and
CD-ROM.

Criminal Law

ROBERT E. CLEARY, JR., KURTZ CRIMINAL OFFENSES AND DEFENSES
IN GEORGIA (2006 ed.). St. Paul, Minn.: Thomson/West. Published annually. Available on Westlaw.

ROBERT E. CLEARY, JR., MOLNAR GEORGIA CRIMINAL LAW: CRIMES
AND PUNISHMENTS (6th ed. 2000 & Supp. 2006). Suwanee, Ga.:
Harrison Co. (a division of Thomson/West). Available on
Westlaw.

GEORGIA PROCEDURE, vols. 9–12 Criminal Procedure (1995 &
Supp. 2006). Rochester, NY: Lawyers Cooperative (a division of
Thomson/West). Available on Westlaw and CD-ROM.

JOHN J. (JACK) GOGER, DANIEL'S GEORGIA CRIMINAL TRIAL PRAC-
TICE (2007 ed.). St. Paul, Minn.: Thomson/West. Published annually. Available on Westlaw.

JOHN J. (JACK) GOGER, DANIEL'S GEORGIA CRIMINAL TRIAL PRAC-
TICE FORMS (6th ed. 2006). St. Paul, Minn.: Thomson/West.
Available on Westlaw and CD-ROM.

JOHN J. (JACK) GOGER, DANIEL'S GEORGIA HANDBOOK ON CRIMI-
NAL EVIDENCE (2006 ed.). St. Paul, Minn.: Thomson/West.
Published annually. Available on Westlaw.

DONALD F. SAMUEL, GEORGIA CRIMINAL LAW CASE FINDER (2006
ed.). 2 vols. Danvers, MA: Matthew Bender, LexisNexis. Published annually.

Damages

ERIC JAMES HERTZ & MARK D. LINK, GEORGIA LAW OF DAMAGES:
WITH FORMS (2007 ed.). St. Paul, Minn.: Thomson/West. Published annually. Available on Westlaw.

ERIC JAMES HERTZ & MARK D. LINK, PUNITIVE DAMAGES IN GEOR-
GIA (2d ed. 2006). St. Paul, Minn.: Thomson/West. Available
on Westlaw.

Debtor and Creditor

Frank S. Alexander, Georgia Real Estate Finance & Foreclosure Law with Forms (4th ed. 2004 & Supp. 2007). St. Paul Minn.: Thomson/West. Available on Westlaw.

Elder Law

Michael S. Reeves, Elder Care and Nursing Home Litigation in Georgia with Forms (2000 & Supp. 2006). Suwanee, Ga.: Harrison Co. (a division of Thomson/West). Alternative title: Long-Term Health Care: Planning Your Golden Years in Georgia. Available on Westlaw.

Eminent Domain

Daniel F. Hinkel, Georgia Eminent Domain (2000 & Supp. 2006). Suwanee, Ga.: Harrison Co. (a division of Thomson/West). Available on Westlaw.

Employment and Labor

See also Workers' Compensation.

Jeffrey L. Hirsch & Roger K. Quillen, Labor and Employment in Georgia: A Guide to Employment Laws, Regulations, and Practices (1999). 2 vols. Loose-leaf. Austin, TX: Butterworth Legal Publishing (a LexisNexis title). Available on LexisNexis.

James W. Wimberly, Georgia Employment Law (3d ed. 2000 & Supp. 2006). Suwanee, Ga.: Harrison Co. (a division of Thomson/West). Available on Westlaw.

Environmental Law

Georgia Conservation Law Handbook (2003). Loose-leaf. Charlottesville, VA: LexisNexis.

Hunton & Williams, Georgia Environmental Law Handbook (3d ed. 2002). Rockville, MD: Government Institutes.

Evidence

Neal W. Dickert, Georgia Handbook on Foundations and Objections (2006 ed.). St. Paul, Minn.: Thomson/West. Available on Westlaw.

John J. (Jack) Goger, Daniel's Georgia Handbook on Criminal Evidence (2006 ed.). St. Paul, Minn.: Thomson/West. Published annually. Available on Westlaw.

Michael E. McLaughlin, Herman & McLaughlin Admissibility of Evidence in Civil Cases: A Manual for Georgia Trial Lawyers (5th ed. 2006). St. Paul, Minn: Thomson/West. Available on Westlaw.

Paul S. Milich, Courtroom Handbook on Georgia Evidence: With Comparisons to the Federal Rules of Evidence (2006 ed.). St. Paul, Minn.: Thomson/West. Published annually. Available on Westlaw.

Paul S. Milich, Georgia Rules of Evidence (2d ed. 2002 & Supp. 2007). St. Paul, Minn.: Thomson/West. Available on Westlaw.

D. Lake Rumsey, Jr., Agnor's Georgia Evidence (3d ed. 1993 & Supp. 2006). Norcross, Ga.: Harrison Co. (a division of Thomson/West). Available on Westlaw.

Alexander Scherr, Green Georgia Law of Evidence (5th ed. 1999 & Supp. 2007). Norcross, Ga.: Harrison Co. (a division of Thomson/West). Available on Westlaw.

Family and Juvenile Law

Edward E. Bates, Jr., Georgia Domestic Relations Forms: Practice (1988) Loose-leaf. Rockville, MD: Matthew Bender, LexisNexis. Available on LexisNexis and Forms on Diskette.

Dan E. McConaughey, Georgia Divorce, Alimony, and Child Custody (2007 ed.). St. Paul, Minn.: Thomson/West. Published annually. Available on Westlaw and CD-ROM.

Barry B. McGough, Georgia Divorce (2005). Loose-leaf. St. Paul, Minn.: Thomson/West.

Mark H. Murphy, Georgia Juvenile Practice and Procedure with Forms, (4th ed. 2001 & Supp. 2006). Suwanee, Ga.: Harrison Co. (a division of Thomson/West). Available on Westlaw.

Kathy L. Portnoy & Charla E. Strawser, Georgia Domestic Relations Case Finder (3d ed. 2004 & Supp. 2006). Newark, NJ: Matthew Bender, LexisNexis. Available on LexisNexis.

Jennifer L. Roberts, William J. Self II & Victoria Ferreira, Georgia Guardian and Ward: An Overview of Guardianships and Conservatorships of Minors and Wards in Georgia (2006 ed.). St. Paul, Minn.: Thomson/West. Available on Westlaw.

Forms

See Collections, Finestone, Hinkel

Corporations, Fischer, Kaplan

Criminal Law, Goger

Damages, Hertz

Debtor and Creditor, Alexander

Elder Law, Reeves

Family and Juvenile Law, Bates, McGough, Murphy

Insurance Law, Jenkins

Landlord and Tenant, Dawkins

Practice and Procedure, McFadden, Purdom (2 titles), Sheppard, Weltner

Probate and Administration of Estates, Levy, Radford, Wise

Real Property, Alexander, Grove, Hinkel (2 titles)

Securities, Rankin

Security Interests, Rankin

Torts and Personal Injury, Gorby, Hertz, Smith

Workers' Compensation, Hood

Wrongful Death, CLEARY

GERALD BLANCHARD, ED., GEORGIA FORMS: LEGAL AND BUSINESS (1994). 5 vols. Loose-leaf. New York: Lawyers Cooperative (a division of Thomson/West). Includes annual paperback Tables & Index volume. Available on Westlaw and CD-ROM.

BROWN'S GEORGIA PLEADING, PRACTICE AND LEGAL FORMS ANNOTATED (2d ed. 1989 & Supp. 2007). 11 vols.; Volumes 4, 7, and 9 are 3d ed. Norcross, Ga.: Harrison Co. (a division of Thomson/West). Available on Westlaw and CD-ROM.

JEFFERSON JAMES DAVIS & MILES E. EASTWOOD, GEORGIA LITIGATION FORMS AND ANALYSIS (1998 & Supp. 2006). 3 vols. Loose-leaf. St. Paul, Minn.: West Group (a division of Thomson/West). Available on Westlaw and CD-ROM.

VICTORIA C. FERREIRA, FORMS FOR PLEADING UNDER THE GEORGIA CIVIL PRACTICE ACT (1997 & Supp. 2007). Norcross, Ga.: Harrison Co. (a division of Thomson/West). Available on Westlaw as part of BROWN'S GA PLEADING, PRACTICE AND LEGAL FORMS ANNOTATED (2d ed).

FELTON A. JENKINS, JR., RALPH A. PITTS & ROBERT R. AMBLER, JR., GEORGIA CIVIL PROCEDURE FORMS (2004). 2 vols. Loose-leaf. Newark, NJ: Matthew Bender, LexisNexis. Available on LexisNexis, CD-ROM, and Forms on Diskette.

RICK RUSKELL, RUSKELL'S CIVIL PLEADING AND PRACTICE FORMS FOR USE WITH WEST'S OFFICIAL CODE OF GEORGIA (6th ed. 2003). 3 vols. Loose-leaf. St. Paul, Minn.: Thomson/West.

General

ANN BLUM & ANNA D. BOLING, AN INTRODUCTION TO LAW IN GEORGIA (4th ed. 2004). State Bar of Georgia, Younger Lawyers Section Staff. Athens, Ga.: Carl Vinson Institute of Government, University of Georgia.

ENCYCLOPEDIA OF GEORGIA LAW (1960 & Supp. 2002). Vols. 1-30. Norcross, Ga.: Harrison Co. (a division of Thomson/West). No longer updated.

Georgia Jurisprudence (1995 & Supp. 2006). 23 vols. St. Paul, Minn.: Thomson/West. Available on Westlaw and CD-ROM.

Byron L. Sparber, Carl H. Cofer, & Thomas A. Ritchie, eds. Southeast Transaction Guide: Florida, Georgia, Alabama (1976). 20 vols. Loose-leaf. New York: Matthew Bender (a division of LexisNexis). Available on LexisNexis and CD-ROM.

Insurance

See also Workers' Compensation.

Frank E. Jenkins III & Wallace Miller III, Georgia Automobile Insurance Law Including Tort Law with Forms (2007). St. Paul, Minn.: Thomson/West. Published annually. Available on Westlaw and CD-ROM.

Jury Instructions

Council of Superior Court Judges of Georgia, Suggested Pattern Jury Instructions (2004). Volume 1: Civil Cases, 4th ed. and Volume 2: Criminal Cases 3d ed. Athens: Carl Vinson Institute of Government, University of Georgia.

Landlord-Tenant Law

William J. Dawkins, Georgia Landlord and Tenant: Breach and Remedies, with Forms (3d ed. 1998 & Supp. 2006). Norcross, Ga.: Harrison Co. (a division of Thomson/West). Available on Westlaw.

James A. Flemming, Georgia Landlord and Tenant: Lease Forms and Clauses (2d ed. 2000 & Supp. 2007). Norcross, Ga.: Harrison Co. (a division of Thomson/West). Available on Westlaw.

Medical Malpractice

C. Ashley Royal et al., Medical Torts in Georgia: A Handbook on State and Federal Law (2006 ed). St. Paul, Minn.: Thomson/West.

Motor Vehicle Law

See also Insurance Law, JENKINS.

WILLIAM C. HEAD, GEORGIA DUI TRIAL PRACTICE MANUAL (2006). St Paul, Minn.: Thomson/West. Available on Westlaw.

GEORGE A. STEIN, GEORGIA DUI LAW: A RESOURCE FOR LAWYERS AND JUDGES (2003 & Supp. 2006). Newark, NJ: Matthew Bender, LexisNexis. Available in LexisNexis.

Practice and Procedure

ALSTON & BIRD LLP, GEORGIA APPELLATE PRACTICE HANDBOOK (5th ed. 2003). Athens, Ga.: Institute of Continuing Legal Education in Georgia.

RONALD L. CARLSON, TRIAL HANDBOOK FOR GEORGIA LAWYERS (3d ed. 2003 & Supp. 2007). St. Paul, Minn.: Thomson/West.

GEORGIA PROCEDURE (1995 & Supp. 2006). 13 vols. (vols. 1-8 Civil Procedure, vols. 9-12 Criminal Procedure) Rochester, NY: Lawyers Cooperative (a division of Thomson/West). Available on Westlaw and CD-ROM.

HARDY GREGORY, JR., GEORGIA CIVIL PRACTICE (3d ed. 2003). Loose-leaf. Newark, NJ: Matthew Bender, LexisNexis. Available in LexisNexis and CD-ROM.

CHRISTOPHER J. McFADDEN, EDWARD C. BREWER III & CHARLES R. SHEPPARD, GEORGIA APPELLATE PRACTICE WITH FORMS (2d ed. 2002 & Supp. 2007). St. Paul, Minn.: Thomson/West. Available on Westlaw.

WAYNE M. PURDOM, GEORGIA CIVIL DISCOVERY WITH FORMS (6th ed. 2001 & Supp. 2006). Suwanee, Ga.: Harrison Co. (a division of Thomson/West). Available on Westlaw.

WAYNE M. PURDOM, GEORGIA MAGISTRATE COURT HANDBOOK WITH FORMS (4th ed. 2002 & Supp. 2007). Suwanee, Ga.: Harrison Co. (a division of Thomson/West). Available on Westlaw.

RICHARD C. RUSKELL, DAVIS & SHULMAN'S GEORGIA PRACTICE & PROCEDURE (2007 ed.). St. Paul, Minn.: Thomson/West. Published annually. Available on Westlaw.

CHARLES R. SHEPPARD, HANDBOOK ON GEORGIA PRACTICE WITH FORMS (2006 ed). St. Paul, Minn.: Thomson/West. Published annually. Available on Westlaw and CD-ROM.

PHILIP WELTNER II, GEORGIA PROCESS AND SERVICE WITH FORMS (2000 & Supp. 2002). Suwanee, Ga.: Harrison Co. (a division of Thomson/West). Available on Westlaw.

Probate and Administration of Estates

BENTRAM L. LEVY & BENJAMIN T. WHITE, GEORGIA ESTATE PLANNING, WILL DRAFTING AND ESTATE ADMINISTRATION FORMS: PRACTICE (1987). 2 vols, Loose-leaf. Rockville, MD: Aspen Pub. (a LexisNexis title). Available on LexisNexis and Forms on Diskette.

MARY F. RADFORD, REDFEARN WILLS & ADMINISTRATION IN GEORGIA (6th ed. 2000 & Supp. 2007). 2 vols. Suwanee, Ga.: Harrison Co. (a division of Thomson/West). Available on Westlaw and Forms on Diskette.

TERESA E. WISE, GEORGIA PROBATE AND ADMINISTRATION WITH FORMS (3d ed. 1998 & Supp. 2006). Norcross, Ga.: Harrison Co. (a division of Thomson/West). Available on Westlaw.

Products Liability

JANE E. THORPE, DAVID R. VENDERBUSH, & J. KENNARD NEAL, GEORGIA PRODUCTS LIABILITY LAW (3d ed. 2002 & Supp. 2006). St. Paul, Minn.: Thomson/West. Available on Westlaw.

Real Property

FRANK S. ALEXANDER, GEORGIA REAL ESTATE FINANCE AND FORECLOSURE LAW WITH FORMS (4th ed. 2004 & Supp. 2007). St. Paul, Minn.: Thomson/West. Available on Westlaw.

Russell S. Grove Jr., Deborah E. Glass, & Bruce P. Cohen, Georgia Real Estate Forms: Practice (1987). 3 vols. Loose-leaf. Rockville, MD: Aspen Pub. (a LexisNexis title). Available on LexisNexis and Forms on diskette.

Daniel F. Hinkel, Abraham Georgia Real Estate Sales Contracts (5th ed. 2000 & Supp. 2007). Suwanee, Ga.: Harrison Co. (a division of Thomson/West). Available on Westlaw.

Daniel F. Hinkel, Georgia Real Estate Title Examinations and Closings with Forms (3d ed. 2002 & Supp. 2007). Suwanee, Ga.: Harrison Co. (a division of Thomson/West). Available on Westlaw.

Daniel F. Hinkel, Pindar's Georgia Real Estate Law and Procedure with Forms (6th ed. 2004 & Supp. 2006). 3 vols. St. Paul, Minn.: Thomson/West. Available on Westlaw and Forms on Diskette.

Seth G. Weissman & Ned Blumenthal, The Red Book on Real Estate Contracts in Georgia (2005). Atlanta, Ga.: Weissman, Nowack, Curry & Wilco, P.C.

Securities

James S. Rankin, Jr., Georgia Securities Practice with Forms (2001). Suwanee, Ga.: Harrison Co. (a division of Thomson/West). Available on Westlaw.

Security Interests

James S. Rankin, Jr., Dobbs' Georgia Enforcement of Security Interests in Personal Property Under Revised Article 9 with Forms (3d ed. 2002 & Supp. 2007). Suwanee, Ga.: Harrison Co. (a division of Thomson/West). Available on Westlaw.

Taxation

Georgia Tax Reports, CCH Tax Research Network (no longer sold in print, but may be available in libraries).

State Tax Group of Alston & Bird, LLP, eds., Guidebook to Georgia Taxes (2007 ed.). Chicago, IL: CCH. Published annually.

Torts and Personal Injury

See also   Insurance, Jenkins

Medical Malpractice, Royal

Charles R. Adams III, Georgia Law of Torts (2007 ed.). St. Paul, Minn.: Thomson/West. Published annually. Available on Westlaw.

Charles R. Adams III & Deron R. Hicks, Georgia Law of Torts: Preparation for Trial (2001 & Supp. 2002). Suwanee, Ga.: Harrison Co. (a division of Thomson/West). Available on Westlaw.

Michael J. Gorby, Premises Liability in Georgia with Forms (1998 & Supp. 2006). Norcross, Ga.: Harrison Co. (a division of Thomson/West). Available on Westlaw.

Eric James Hertz, Mark D. Link, & Houston D. Smith III, Georgia Law of Torts Forms (2002). St. Paul, Minn.: Thomson/West. Available on Westlaw.

Houston D. Smith III, Soft Tissue Injuries in Georgia Including Whiplash, with Forms (1998 & Supp. 2006). Norcross, Ga.: Harrison Co. (a division of Thomson/West). Available on Westlaw.

Workers' Compensation

James B. Heirs & Robert R. Potter, Georgia Workers' Compensation: Law and Practice (5th ed. 2007). St. Paul Minn.: Thomson/West. Available on Westlaw.

Jack B. Hood, Benjamin A. Hardy Jr., & Bobby Lee Cook, Georgia Workers' Compensation Claims with Forms (4th ed. 2001 & Supp. 2006). Suwanee, Ga.: Harrison Co. (a division of Thomson/West). Available on Westlaw.

RICHARD C. KISSIAH, KISSIAH'S GEORGIA WORKERS' COMPENSA-
TION LAW (3d ed. 2006). 2 vols. Newark, NJ: Matthew Bender,
LexisNexis. Available on LexisNexis.

Wrongful Death

ROBERT E. CLEARY, ELDRIDGE'S GEORGIA WRONGFUL DEATH AC-
TIONS WITH FORMS (3d ed. 1998 & Supp. 2007). Norcross, Ga.:
Harrison Co. (a division of Thomson/West). Available on
Westlaw.

About the Authors

Nancy P. Johnson is Law Librarian and Professor of Law at the Georgia State University College of Law Library in Atlanta, Georgia.

Elizabeth G. Adelman is Head of Collection Management at the University at Buffalo Law Library in Buffalo, NY. Formerly, she was Head of Public Services and Instructor of Law at the Georgia State University College of Law Library in Atlanta, Georgia.

Nancy J. Adams is the U.S. District Court Librarian for the Northern District of Georgia in Atlanta, Georgia. Formerly, she was Senior Reference Librarian at the Georgia State University College of Law Library in Atlanta, Georgia.

Index